THE DEVIL DOGS AT BELLEAU WOOD

U.S. MARINES IN WORLD WAR I

DICK CAMP

ZENITH PRESS

Copyright © 2008 by Dick Camp

First Published in 2008 by Zenith Press, an imprint of The Quarto Group, 100 Cummings Center, Suite 265-D, Beverly, MA 01915, USA. T (978) 282-9590 F (978) 283-2742 QuartoKnows.com

Zenith Press titles are also available at discount for retail, wholesale, promotional, and bulk purchase. For details, contact the Special Sales Manager by email at specialsales@quarto.com or by mail at The Quarto Group, Attn: Special Sales Manager, 100 Cummings Center, Suite 265-D, Beverly, MA 01915, USA.

Editor: Scott Pearson
Designer: Christopher Fayers

Library of Congress Cataloging-in-Publication Data

Camp, Richard D.
   The Devil Dogs at Belleau Wood : U.S. Marines in World War I / by Dick Camp.
      p. cm.
   Includes bibliographical references.
   ISBN-13: 978-0-7603-3189-7 (pbk.)
   ISBN-10: 0-7603-3189-8 (pbk.)
   1. Belleau Wood, Battle of, France, 1918. 2. United States. Marine Corps—History—World War, 1914-1918. 3. World War, 1914-1918—Regimental histories—United States. I. Title.
D545.B4C36 2008
940.4'34—dc22

2007039557

About the Author:

Dick Camp is a retired Marine Corps colonel and the author of *Lima-6*, the critically acclaimed Vietnam War memoir of his service as a Marine infantry company commander at Khe Sanh. He is also the author of three previous works of military history from Zenith Press, *Battleship Arizona's Marines at War*, *Iwo Jima Recon*, and *Leatherneck Legends: Conversations with the Marine Corps' Old Breed*. Camp is currently the vice president for museum operations at the Marine Corps Heritage Foundation, which, in conjunction with the Marine Corps, oversees the National Museum of the Marine Corps. Camp resides in northern Virginia.

On the cover: A 37mm gun crew from Headquarters Company, 6th Marines, in the dense, heavily shelled Argonne Forest in the fall of 1918; these were the same conditions they had faced in Belleau Wood in June, which lay less than a hundred miles to the east. *National Archives*

On the frontispiece: The Marine Corps quickly capitalized on the "Devil Dog" nickname by producing a recruiting poster. *Marine Corps History Division*

On the title pages: Marine combat artist Tom Lovell's rendition of the attack in Belleau Wood. *Marine Corps History Division*

On the back cover: Cleaning out machine-gun nests in Belleau Wood. *Frank E. Schoonover*

Contents

Sergeants Clint Owens and Michael Ervin represent U.S. Marine buglers past and present in a 2006 memorial ceremony at the Aisne-Marne Cemetery, in Belleau, France, where 2,289 U.S. service members lay at rest. The surrounding French countryside was the site of a pivotal battle of World War I, the last major German offensive of the war. The battle, which halted the German advance toward Paris, was gruesome and bloody, and record Marine Corps casualties would not be topped until the recapture of Tarawa in November 1943. *Staff Sgt. Will Price, USMC*

Preface

Some years ago I was on leave at my parents' home in upper New York. With little to do except get fat from my mother's cooking, I decided to try and locate a former Marine in Rochester, an hour's drive away. It was a spur of the moment thing. I didn't have a phone number, only an address—almost a fool's errand. Surprisingly, I found the modest house in an older section of the city. I took the chance that he was home and rang the doorbell. After some moments the door opened and an older gentleman peered out, a look of genuine surprise on his face as he scrutinized my Marine officer's green uniform. I explained the purpose of my visit—and he was kind enough to invite me in.

We went into his living room, and for the next two hours, Mr. Robert Benedict, former private, 82nd Company, 6th Marine Regiment, regaled me with stories of his service in France during the "Great War." Despite being well into his seventh decade of life, his account was lucid and rich in detail—delivered in a matter-of-fact manner, without false bravado. He described coming of age during the realistic combat training in the harsh winter and spring of 1918. As warm weather lightened spirits, rumors swept the ranks that the Germans were on the move. Bob became more animated as he related the feeling of excitement during the forced march to the front. I believe in his mind's eye he saw again those long lines of green uniformed youngsters striding confidently forward. He quite proudly told me how his company commander picked him to be a runner, a mark of honor.

Bob related how his company reached a wood and formed an assault formation. On signal, they advanced by platoon, line abreast, beyond the tree line into an open field of waist-high wheat. Just then his voice caught, and he struggled to continue. I broke in, hoping to give him time to recover. "Where were you?" I asked. After a long moment, he replied, "Why, it was Belleau Wood." Bob excused himself and said, "I can't go on, it's too painful, too many upsetting memories."

A chill went up my spine, as the realization hit me that the old man sitting across from me was the living embodiment of the Corps' mystique—*Belleau Wood* was synonymous with *Marine valor and sacrifice*—that is instilled in every new Marine.

Years later, I invited Gen. Lemuel C. Shepherd, the retired twentieth commandant of the Marine Corps, to attend a meeting of my junior officers at the San Diego Officer's Club. The "old man" totally captivated them, as he talked about his forty-two years of active service. An officer asked a final question. "General, what was the worst thing you faced during your four decades of service?" Shepherd did not miss a beat, "Machine guns at Belleau Wood."

I remembered those incidents as if they were yesterday. Those two old men were my link with the old Corps—and in a fashion, they forged a link between their generation and mine. The history of the Corps, in many respects, is an oral account of the past, as told by one Marine to another. In a sense, *The Devil Dogs at Belleau Wood* is a "written" oral history.

Well-known artist Howard Chandler Christy's stylized recruiting poster. *Marine Corps History Division*

Chapter 1

WAR!

Hundreds of flag-waving Washingtonians lined the streets from the White House to Capitol Hill waiting to catch a glimpse of President Woodrow Wilson as he made his way to address a joint session of Congress. The jingle of equipment and the striking of steel-shod hooves on the pavement announced the arrival of his entourage. A squadron of mounted cavalry from the garrison at Fort Meyers surrounded the president's carriage. A nervous secretary of war had ordered the armed escort because of a concern for Wilson's safety.

Passions were riding high. More than a thousand demonstrators from the Emergency Peace Foundation descended on the capitol. Groups of them waylaid members of Congress in the corridors. Senator Henry Cabot Lodge had a violent disagreement with one particularly aggressive protester and was assaulted. It was reported that the aging legislator gave as good as he got. "I am glad that I hit him," an unrepentant Lodge related. "The senators all appeared to be perfectly delighted with my having done so."

War fever gripped the country, forcing the president to throw off the cloak of neutrality after a series of provocative German "crimes against humanity," culminating in the sinking of three unarmed American merchant ships—*City of Memphis, Illinois,* and *Vigilancia*—by enemy U-boats (submarines). Fifteen seamen were lost. Wilson strode through the congressional chamber's jam-packed aisle to the podium. "In a low, dispassionate voice . . . he recounted the German outrages, the spying, the sabotage, and the barbarities of submarine attacks." At one point he spoke the phrase that came to frame America's war aim, "Keep the world safe for democracy," which brought the entire assembly to its feet in a roar of approval. Later, in a conversation with his private secretary, Wilson anguished over his comments, "My message today was a message of death for our young men."

Two days later, on Good Friday, a messenger arrived at the White House bearing the war resolution. The somber president slipped into the usher's room off the main lobby of the White House, took pen in hand, and scribbled "Approved 6 April, 1917—Woodrow Wilson" on the document that lay open on the highly polished walnut table. It stated that "the state of war between the United States and the Imperial German Government which has been thrust upon the United States is hereby formally declared." The head usher pressed a buzzer, which sounded in the executive office. A navy aide, Lt. Byron McCandless, ran out onto the White House lawn and used his arms as a semaphore to signal a fellow officer peering out a window of the Navy Department office across the street. A coded message was immediately flashed to every ship and shore installation: "W . . . A . . . R."

Within hours, at 0630 (Guam time) April 6, 1917, a prize crew of Marines, under the command

"WELL, YOUNG MAN, HAVE YOU COME TO JOIN THE MARINES?"

"Volunteer." *Morgan Dennis, featured in* Sergeant Ted Cole, United States Marines *by Everett Tomlinson*

of Lt. W. A. Hall, U.S. Navy, made their way toward the German cruiser SMS *Cormoran* to demand her surrender. The *Cormoran* had been interned in the harbor of Guam, with its crew on board, after fleeing from a British-led naval force. The Americans spotted a German barge headed toward the cruiser. Lieutenant Hall ordered a Marine to fire across the bow with his rifle as a signal to heave to. "The shot, as I recall was fired by Cpl. Michael B. Chockie," Hall recalled, "the noncommissioned officer in charge." This simple act allowed the Marines to lay claim to having fired the first shot of war. A short time later, the Germans set off demolition charges in the *Cormoran's* bottom, sinking her within minutes. Seven German sailors died—America was at war.

Crack Yale Athletes Join Marine Corps

New Haven, Conn., May 8, 1917. Five of Yale's leading athletes, of whom four have captained Yale teams, are today enrolled for service with the Marines. They are Harry Le Gore, the baseball captain and football star; Holcomb York, of the hockey team; Louis Ferguson, who captained one of Yale's best swimming teams; and Johnny Overton,* the track and cross-country team captain and cross-country inter-collegiate champion. All four will receive temporary commissions. Rex Hutchinson, the football center and baseball outfielder, has also joined the Marine Corps.

* Lieutenant John W. Overton was killed in action on July 19, 1918. Major Robert L. Denig wrote, "Overton was hit by a big piece of shell and fell. Afterwards I heard that he was hit in the heart, so his death was without pain. He was buried that night."

Lieutenant Colonel Frederick M. "Fritz" Wise, commanding officer, 2nd Battalion, 5th Marines, recipient of the Army and Navy Distinguished Service Medal. Wise was old Corps, a hard-nosed martinet, whose temper was legendary. He once had the band play "He Was Always in the Way" at the funeral of a troublesome Marine. One lieutenant thought the stocky Wise looked "seven months pregnant." *Marine Corps History Division*

Call to the Colors

Newspaper headlines across the country screamed "WAR," sending the nation's collective blood pumping. The strident *New Orleans Times-Picayune* brayed "This nation, forced at last by brutal aggression and outrage to take up the sword, will wage the war in its own and humanity's defense." Thousands of young men streamed to the colors.

"Ore-passers in Ashtabula, lumbermen in Bangor, cow-punchers in Cheyenne, cotton-farmers in Dallas, miners in Leadville, shoe-workers in Lynn, sophomores in New Haven," wrote Capt. John Thomason, "grocery-clerks in Syracuse, apple-growers in Walla Walla, city boys from Third Avenue, country boys from Bear Notch, youths, black and of alien birth, every type and condition of man between twenty-one and thirty to be found in the country." Marine major Frederic Wise, who was slated to command a battalion in France, said, "They [volunteers] came from universities and clubs, from factories and farms, from garages and shops. Every phase of American life was represented, and all of the best."

In a fit of patriotic fervor, Yale undergraduate Samuel W. Meek joined the throng. "We all felt that great wrong had been done by the Germans, and we wanted to pitch in and help. I think every member of my fraternity went into one branch of the service or another; it just never entered out heads to stay out." Meek volunteered for the Marines after a recruiter talked to the school's dean. "If Yale would furnish a list of ten men with leadership qualifications, the Corps would immediately

Edward A. "Eddie" Craig did not serve in France, much to his regret. Instead he fought in the Banana Wars and later in World War II and Korea, achieving distinction as a consummate combat leader. He retired in 1952 as a lieutenant general, after serving thirty-five years. *Author's collection*

General Lemuel C. "Lem" Shepherd steadily advanced in rank and responsibility. In World War II, he commanded a brigade and a division, in Korea he was the senior Marine in the Pacific, and he ended his forty-two-year career as commandant of the Marines. *Marine Corps History Division*

send them down to their new base at Quantico for officer's training." The dean complied. "We all accepted," Meek said, "and just like that, the Marines had ten new second lieutenants."

Twenty-year-old St. John's Military Academy student Edward A. "Eddie" Craig was another volunteer. "When World War I broke out, I immediately set out to get in the service. I was in school at the time, and on my own. I couldn't get in the Army until I was twenty-one with a commission . . . and twenty in the Marine Corps. Having had ROTC training for four years, I was offered a commission in the Marine Corps." Craig sent a telegram to his army doctor father. "I'm entering the U.S. Marine Corps. I have a chance for a commission. I received a telegram from him: 'Do not join the U.S. Marines under any circumstance. A terrible bunch of drunks and bums,' signed,

Father." Despite the admonition, Craig accepted the commission and thirty-four years later retired from the Corps as a lieutenant general.

Virginia Military Institute senior Lemuel C. Shepherd volunteered because he had seen Maj. Gen. George Barnett, the commandant of the Marine Corps. "General Barnett wore his full dress uniform and had a very snappy aide de camp with him." Within days of the declaration of war, Shepherd and several classmates were headed for Washington to take the commissioning physical. They appeared before the improbably named Capt. Bobo Dessez, USN, the senior member of the medical examining board, a rough, gruff, seagoing bull:

> This old doctor, he just thumped us a few times, checked a few things, and kind of smiled: "Get down over there and stick up your ass.
>
> "Ever have the clap, Shepherd?" he asked, examining my posterior.
>
> "No sir," I replied rather indignantly, having come from a proper Virginia family.
>
> "Turn around," he ordered brusquely, ignoring my response. "Have you ever had piles?"
>
> "No sir."
>
> "You'll do, Shepherd, you'll do."

Colonel Albertus W. Catlin at age forty-nine was a powerfully built man of medium height with iron-gray hair. As a first lieutenant, he commanded the Marine detachment aboard the USS *Maine* at the time of its 1898 sinking in Havana Harbor. In 1914 he commanded the provisional regiment at Vera Cruz, where he was awarded the Congressional Medal of Honor. Severely wounded at Belleau Wood, he was medically retired in 1919 as a brigadier general. *Marine Corps History Division*

Brigadier General Albertus W. Catlin, commanding officer of the 6th Marines wrote: "Sixty percent of the entire regiment—mark this—sixty percent of them were college men. Two-thirds of one entire company came straight from the University of Minnesota." Marine historian Lt. Col. Clyde H. Metcalf wrote, "Three hundred students from the University of Minnesota enlisted en bloc."

First to Fight

On the day war was declared, the total strength of the Marine Corps consisted of 419 officers and 13,000 enlisted men. Less than a month later, Congress voted to expand the Corps to a wartime strength of 31,000—"larger than the regular army

Recruiters resorted to all sorts of gimmicks to advertise. In this case, an elephant from the Barnum & Bailey circus got into the act. *Marine Corps History Division*

New York City recruiting sergeant Michael Fitzgerald, the epitome of a spit-and-polish old-breed Marine. Three stripes on his shoulder mark his rank, while the three stripes on his forearm denote twelve years of service. He also wears a rifle sharpshooter badge on his blouse. What red-blooded American could withstand Fitzgerald's call to the colors? *Marine Corps History Division*

War! A swarm of patriotic Americans flocked to the enlistment stations. Here a Marine recruiting sergeant of sixteen years service (four service stripes on his uniform cuffs—each represents four years) reviews a recruiting bulletin with a prospect applicant. *Marine Corps History Division*

at the beginning of the Spanish American War." The Corps launched a recruiting campaign, featuring the slogan "First to fight," capitalizing on the general desire to get overseas. Columbia University graduate Melvin L. Krulewitch "had heard tales about his grandfather who served in the Civil War. I had no intention of doing anything but getting in the war. I talked with my friends about the service branches. What would be best for me? The buses were going along Fifth Avenue and Riverside Drive, right close to Columbia—the two-decker buses—and on them a sign said *Join The Marines, First To Fight.*"

Hundreds of highly qualified men stormed the recruiting stations, many times more applicants than could be accepted. Marine historian Col. Robert Debs Heinl wrote, "So many high-spirited young men volunteered that, by 4 June 1917, General Barnett closed down on officer appointments from civilian life and, for the rest of the

war, filled the officer corps from the rich talent in the ranks." Applicant Merwin H. Silverthorn described how "the line extended up the office, down the hall, and down four flights of steps, down on the sidewalk, and around the corner."

With so many men to choose from, enlistment standards were rigidly adhered to. An applicant had to "be not less than five feet five inches, nor more than six feet two inches in height; weigh not less than 130 pounds; . . . not less than 18 nor more than 36 years of age; be able to speak, read, and write the English language with ease; native born or naturalized citizen of the United States; steady and regular habits; unmarried, with no one wholly dependent upon him for support; of good health, strong constitution, well formed, sound as to senses and limbs, and not addicted to the use of intoxicants or drugs."

Shepherd was afraid he wouldn't be accepted. "I was underweight because I ran on the track team

General View of Camp. No 2.

An island of hastily erected wooden structures and rows of tents marked the recruits' entire world. They would not see "civilization" until they completed training. This photo shows tables where the recruits would lay out and clean their clothes and equipment. The men in the lower right corner are in the process of "squaring away" their gear. *Marine Corps History Division*

and I was pretty thin in those days." However, the head of the examining board certified that "you young gentlemen have all passed your physical examination." Silverthorn cheated: "Knowing that I probably couldn't pass the eye examination, I memorized the chart."

Making Marines

Shepherd, Silverthorn, Krulewitch, and thousands of others soon found themselves on the way to Parris Island, an insect-infested spit of swampland off the coast from Port Royal, South Carolina. It was an isolated outpost, "a mass of acreage covered

Attentive recruits are given an indoctrination lecture on the dos and don'ts of the recruit depot. The dress of the recruits suggests that many of them were college men who joined out of a sense of patriotism. It would be a few days until the men would be given uniforms. In the meantime, they had to wear what they had when they arrived. *Author's collection*

The tug is loaded to the gunnels with happy new Marines making the perilous trip from Parris Island to the mainland. The wide expanse of open water, threat of snakes, and other "denizens of the deep" discouraged the uncommitted from going over the hill. *Marine Corps History Division*

"You'll be sorry!" Young enlistees approaching the Parris Island landing, soon to be entrusted into the tender mercies of the drill instructors. Their smiling, cheerful faces will soon be replaced by a "thousand-yard stare," as realization sets in— Parris Island is not a vacation resort. *Marine Corps History Division*

with stunted scrub pine, a wind-blown, sandy land utterly bereft of physical comforts," that could be reached only by boat.

One new recruit lamented, "I thought they had landed us on an island for the insane; but later I was told it was the old quarantine camp." Another, Pvt. Sheldon R. Gearhart, wrote his folks, "You know this island is nothing but sand, sand, sand. You can grit your teeth any time, I don't care when, and grate on it. It's in your chow, on the sheets, and in your eyes. It blows and drifts just like snow, and it's just like snow to walk through—you sink in."

"P.I.," as it was called by generations of Marines, was one of four officer-training facilities in 1917. Two were located in California, at Mare Island (near San Francisco) and San Diego, and another at the Marine Corps rifle range at Winthrop, Maryland. Parris Island was also one of two primary recruit training depots for enlisted men. The other was located at Mare Island. Two temporary camps were established at Philadelphia and Norfolk Navy Yard to handle the surge of recruits, but Parris Island handled the lion's share. As a rule, applicants east of the Mississippi River were sent to Parris Island, and those west of the Mississippi were sent to Mare Island. Krulewitch "got on the Charleston & Western Carolina Railroad to go from Savannah to Port Royal to Parris Island. We went across on a barge, and as we came near the entrance, all of those fellows who had come into the Marine Corps a day or two before, and were thus old-timers, hollered to us, 'Shit out of luck, S.O.L., shit out of luck.' "

The Drill Instructor

[Drill instructors were the] old Marines, the tall, straight, mustached professionals who dressed their pride in gaudy blue uniforms, decorated their bodies with salty tattoos, fed their thirst with chewing tobacco, frequently dipped snuff, assuaged fatigue with whiskey, cursed with the metric vigor of Kipling, drilled their troops night and day, held frequent and demanding inspections, and knew everything there was to know about the Springfield .03 rifle.

—Captain Robert B. Asprey, former U.S. Marine,
At Belleau Wood

Upon arrival, the youngsters were turned over to veteran noncommissioned officers who quickly introduced them to their hardcore training methods. "My drill instructor was satisfied with nothing short of perfection," Pvt. Carl Andrew Brannen remembered. "He flew into a rage . . . because we were not doing well on drill. Many times the air almost turned blue with the things he said."

Recruit Malcolm D. Aitken wrote, "The first day at camp I was afraid that I was going to die. The next two weeks my sole fear was that I wasn't going to die. And after, I knew that I'd never die because I'd become so hard that nothing could kill me."

Another recruit recognized Parris Island for what it was. "The island should not be visualized

Two recruits mugging for the camera assume the proper "on guard" stance, knees slightly bent and bayonet point neck high. They are sparring with the .03 rifle tipped with an eighteen-inch bayonet and are wearing cartridge belts that hold one hundred rounds of ammunition in five-round stripper clips. *Marine Corps History Division*

as an island of total gloom and grim torture, but as a place where sissies and boys are made into men. A place where people on leaving have few regrets, but admire, respect, and appreciate the products of its labor. The island is a workshop and not a playground for pleasure-seeking playboys. [It is] a tough school that turns out tough graduates."

Recruits received "not less than eight weeks of preliminary training that qualified them for general service. Krulewitch found that "boot training was very severe—one day work, one day drill. The work that we did was work that would stagger an ordinary person. People said that the [French] Foreign Legion and other military units couldn't

Rifle calisthenics build up the arms and shoulders. After several minutes of lifting the eight-pound .03 rifle waist high, and then over one's head in Parris Island's sweltering heat, even the toughest recruit's muscles would tire. Note the drill instructor (at left) carrying a large swagger stick that he used to emphasize a point. *Author's collection*

Recruits practice firing in the kneeling position, one of four they will learn: standing, kneeling, sitting, and prone. The men on camp stools are coaches helping recruits hit the target's black V-ring for the highest points. *Marine Corps History Division*

Recruits train in the sitting position, rifle slings cinched around the left arm for a steadier grip. The range NCO is at the rear wearing a straw hat and carrying a bullhorn. The Corps considered shooting its reason for existence, and a private could earn $5 extra per month for shooting *expert*—a princely sum in 1917. *Marine Corps History Division*

"We made it!" Graduation and a trip off "Devil's Island." These youngsters will form the 5th and 6th regiments and the 6th Machine Gun Battalion of the 4th Marine Brigade. In France they will face the war-hardened veterans of the Kaiser's killing machine. *Marine Corps History Division*

compare to the early Marine Corps training that we had there."

Private Paradis spent "days learning to get in formation . . . marching back and forth . . . learning how to do squads right and left, and how to handle our rifles and how to care for them. It was blistering hot daytime and cold at night. We were finally whipped into shape for our first hike. We rolled our packs . . . with all our worldly possessions and started across the island about ten or twelve miles. It was a very hot day and some of the boys had a hard time . . . only sheer grit and determination kept them going." The recruits quickly toughened up, as they moved through the training schedule. "We were taught to maneuver," Paradis recalled, "going from platoon formation to company formation then to column and wave formation. After a month of this sort of drill we went to the rifle range."

The recruits spent two weeks on the rifle range, learning to shoot the bolt action .03 rifle, the Corps' raison d'etre. Private Roland Rogers wrote, "Next week we go on the rifle range, and believe me, I am going into it for all there is in me, because it means a whole lot to a person if they qualify as an expert rifleman."

The Corps' emphasis on shooting was a source of great pride according to Catlin, with Secretary of the Navy Josephus Daniels announcing, "Their [Marines] sharpshooting . . . has amazed soldiers of European armies, accustomed merely to shooting in the general direction of the enemy. Under the fiercest fire the Marines calmly adjusted their sights, aimed for their man, and killed him."

"It was a happy and exuberant bunch of men [upon graduation], for we were glad to get off the hell-hole called Parris Island." The new Marines were sent to the Overseas Depot at Quantico, Virginia, for advanced infantry training before shipping out to France. The six-thousand-acre site was an ideal location for training—deep-

Hastily built wooden barracks, crammed together on muddy ground near the Potomac River. With the pine forest cleared from the hillsides, water ran off directly into the base. In winter, wind whistled through the shoddy barracks. Comfort was not considered—the men were quickly trained then formed into companies, battalions, and regiments for immediate assignment overseas. *Marine Corps History Division*

water approaches for transports, main railroad line, and enough space for thousands of men to practice the art of war—except for:

> Mud, mud, mud
> Hop, slip, and thud
> Unadulterated mud.

In August 1917, Marine engineers struggled to clear the heavily forested land and create a training base. Second Lieutenant W. B. Jackson arrived in the middle of the night. "[There] were few streets or sidewalks and much, much mud. We stayed in an unoccupied wooden shack. We had no blankets, so we spent the night lying on one cot mattress for a bed and using another cot mattress for cover."

Second Lieutenant James McBrayer Sellers described the new encampment. "Looks like pictures of mining towns which I have seen. There is one small street which constitutes the original town. This street leads right up from the pier. . . . There are rows and rows of unpainted wooden shacks. . . . The small streets between are all cut up with rain wash, and we stumble over what is left of a former small forest, roots and stumps, and sewer excavations."

Eddy Craig arrived at a time when "the base was a big mud hole. I remember the day I reported. There were trucks struck all along Barnett Avenue and the stumps sticking out all over had not been taken out."

Ladies of the Evening

Construction wasn't the only round-the-clock activity according to newly commissioned 2nd Lt. William A. Worton. "Quantico was full of prostitutes because of the thousands of construction workers." The base commander decided to run the "girls" out, and turned to Worton, the officer of the day. "He'd issued an order to put them on the train for Washington. We sent the MPs in there on Tuesday around ten o'clock in the morning—if we'd gone in there Saturday, we'd had a fight with the construction workers. We lined up about a hundred of the girls and took them to the railroad station, where I bought their tickets." Young Worton didn't see two of his old-time sergeants whispering to one of the girls. "As the train rolled in, about six of them came over and kissed me good-bye, 'Goodbye sweetheart,' and all waved as they boarded the train. GOD! The NCOs had set me up. I was mad as hell as I marched the detachment back and reported to the base commander. He'd heard all about it and said, 'I understand you gave them a grand send off, young man. Somebody told me they were kissing you right and left. You been running down there and looking those girls over every night?' I was furious."

Second Lieutenant Graves B. Erskine lamented that "Barnett Avenue was a mire of mud. They ran a truck down the avenue one day and it got stuck. They sent the other (only two trucks at the base) and it got stuck. So, all the trucks in the Marine Corps were stuck on Barnett Avenue! Two teams of mules were sent over to haul them out."

Quantico seemed like a boom town. Erskine thought there were as many as ten thousand work-men there. "You could hear the hammers going all night long, it was a round-the-clock operation."

Barracks consisted of rough-hewn board shacks that barely kept out the weather. Craig was assigned to one of the poorly built huts that served as officer's quarters. "The cracks had no batting over them, which allowed the wind and rain to come through. When winter came, it was pretty cold . . . unless you sat by the stove in the center

Under the supervision of instructors, Marines dug miles of field works. Sticks and braces become a wicker siding to hold the banks of a freshly dug trench. Duckboards would be laid in the bottom of the trench to keep the men's feet dry. Once the trench was finished, the men would practice attacking and defending them. In France they would learn to dig while lying down and being shot at—one can get underground quickly with the right incentive. *Marine Corps History Division*

A practice attack with fixed bayonets. Unfortunately, this formation was easy prey for the German machine gunners, although at Belleau Wood, the gutsy Marines were able to penetrate their positions—but at great cost. *Marine Corps History Division*

of the room. The rooms also had open cracks, which the wind and rain came through."

Private Al Appenheimer, 1st Machine Gun Battalion, lived in the enlisted barracks. "The men are quartered in bunk houses holding fifty men each. As you step in the door at either end there is a row of 25 cots on either side of a central isle. On the foot of each cot is hung the occupant's pack carrier, which when he is out for duty carries his mess kit, blanket, poncho, change of clothes, and toilet articles . . . a seabag under his cot holds his personal effects . . . his extra shoes, neatly shined, lay at the foot of his cot, and his rifle, suspended by two cords, is on the right side." Appenheimer found the camp to be comfortable, despite the mud, and wrote home saying, "If things are made much more comfortable the fellows will hate to leave, even though they know that there is a chance to lick the Dutchmen [Germans]."

Quantico's main purpose was to prepare Marines for combat. "The training was rugged," Craig remembered. "Each morning before daylight, we were out for setting-up exercises, then rifle calisthenics, and this was followed by a run in company formation under arms to the old railroad station and back. I found that by breakfast time I was so tired that I could not eat very much. Then by nine or ten in the morning I would be ravenous."

The training was realistic and often taught by French and British veterans. "We constructed a complete trench system as learned from the war in Europe." The men dug miles of revetted trenches, bombproof shelters, and posts of command (PC). A miniature battlefield was created: "a bit of Flanders in Virginia."

An NCO in the mines and sappers wrote proudly, "I am at Chateau-Thierry! Not the one in France, but a regular imitation right here in Virginia. A whole section of the Virginia woodland has been taken over and blasted, dug, and mined . . . until it is almost an exact replica of the country around Chateau-Thierry. Troops of Marines come through here before going to France and help dig the trenches and take part in sham battles and patrol raids."

Eddy Craig related how the "boys" sometimes got a little carried away. "Raids were conducted by Marines armed with wooden rifles, tennis balls over the bayonets to prevent injury, to capture prisoners from the defenders." Marines being Marines, exuberance was the order of the day and "many times the tennis balls would be accidentally removed.

Prisoners were often removed in a limp condition."

Corporal H. B. Field, 18th Company, 5th Marines, lamented, "We worked long and hard in the very hottest time of the year. Not a day went by but what we would come in after drill wet to the skin with perspiration. And here too we got a taste of modern warfare, such as bayonet fighting, hand grenade throwing, and last but by no means least, digging a set of real trenches, many of which we would soon see and live in." Long hours were spent in bayonet drills, using bags of straw hanging on wires.

Corporal Don V. Paradis "attacked them as a Marine manipulated the bag with a long pole. I remember one of the orders was to always twist your rifle as you pulled it out from a body, otherwise it might stick."

James Sellers said there were "dummies all over for bayonet practice, and at all hours of the day, enlisted men can be seen slaughtering these dummy Germans."

Officers were not immune from hard work. W. B. Jackson "was given a training course in building concrete pillbox machine-gun emplacements. We hauled the stuff for a quarter mile, trying to be as quiet as possible. If our instructors heard us, they blew whistles, signifying enemy machine guns—'twas different and fun." One bit of training that all officers and enlisted men shared equally was a "taste" of gas. Men were issued awkward box-type gas masks, taught how to put them on, and taken through a hut filled with smoke to simulate gas. Unfortunately, the training was not realistic, and the men did not take it seriously, which would prove damaging out on the battlefields of France.

THE LEATHERNECK

An artist's rendition of a Marine about to "spit" an enemy. At the time, great emphasis was placed on bayonet fighting to teach the men to be aggressive. The French were great believers in the bayonet—but the introduction of the machine gun made it an obsolete weapon. *Morgan Dennis, featured in* Dear Folks at Home*, edited by Kemper Cowing and Courtney Riley Cooper*

"First to Fight" recruiting poster. *Marine Corps History Division*

Chapter 2

Transportation Has Been Arranged

The fact that Marines were going to France at all was solely through the unremitting effort of the major general commandant, George Barnett, who launched a personal campaign to convince the secretary of war, Newton D. Baker, to use his Marines. Barnett recalled, "We had used the slogan 'First to Fight' on our [recruiting] posters, and I didn't want that slogan made ridiculous." Despite a shortage of trained men, the army did not want Marines and dredged up phony roadblocks, which in the cold light of day proved to be groundless.

George Barnett, the major general commandant, in full dress uniform of the period. Barnett and his wife were socially prominent Washingtonians who were politically connected to the city's elite. General Barnett saw the war in France as something the Corps had to participate in—or the Corps would forever be relegated to small detachments aboard ships. *Marine Corps History Division*

Barnett, a socially prominent Washington insider, enlisted the aid of the president. Woodrow Wilson ordered the secretary of war, "In pursuance of the authority vested in me by law, it is hereby directed that you issue the necessary orders detaching for service with the Army a force of Marines to be known as the Fifth Regiment of Marines."

The secretary penned a note to Barnett with one last ploy. "I am sorry to have to tell you that it will be utterly impossible for the War Department to furnish transportation for a Marine Regiment with the first outfit sailing. . . ." General Barnett had an ace up his sleeve. A friend and ally, Adm. W. S. Benson, chief of naval operations, had "reserved" three navy transports for the Marines. Barnett wrote Secretary Baker, rather tongue-in-cheek, "Please give yourself no further trouble in this matter, as transportation for the Marines has been arranged."

The 2nd Battalion, 5th Marine Regiment, was one of the first units organized for service in France. Its commander, Maj. Frederic May "Fritz" Wise, was described as "a queer combination of ability and hard-headedness, an even-tempered man who was mad all the time. He was always rough on his men and the nemesis of junior officers." Lem Shepherd, a platoon commander in the 55th Company said that "Wise was an old-time Marine, who entered the Corps before the turn of the century and saw his first action during the Boxer Rebellion." Marines poured into Philadelphia to join the battalion. Newly minted Leathernecks were joined by several hundred veterans, long-service men, who were brought back from expeditionary duty in Haiti, Cuba, and Santo Domingo. Units were quickly formed and marched to the train stations. Catlin remarked that in the 6th Marines, "The officers, from captain up, and fifty or so of the noncommissioned officers were old-time Marines, but the junior officers and privates were all new men."

John Thomason wrote poetically, "There were also a number of diverse people who ran curiously to type, with drilled shoulders and a bone-deep sunburn, and a tolerant scorn of nearly everything on earth. Their speech was flavored with navy words, and words culled from all the folk who live on the seas and the ports where warships go. They drank the eau de vie of Haute-marne, and reminisced on saki, and vino, and Bacardi rum—strange drinks in

Boarding a train in full marching order—carrying the .03 rifle, sheathed bayonet, a cartridge belt, packs containing an extra uniform, wool blanket, mess kit, bacon tin, "silverware," sewing kit, and, if there was room, small amounts of personal items. Leggings keep their trousers tucked in. They are wearing the campaign cover—in today's parlance, a "Smokey Bear Hat." *Marine Corps History Division*

Traveling in style, except the passenger cars are jammed with men, equipment, and weapons. But it's better than hiking, and Marines show their glee at not having to travel by shank's mare. *Marine Corps History Division*

John W. Thomason Jr., noted author, illustrator, and one of the Corps' first combat artists, served as an infantry officer in the 6th Marines at Belleau Wood. His drawings would grace the pages of the *Saturday Evening Post* as well as other popular magazines of the day. A prolific writer, his well-received books showed the country the spirit of the Marine Corps. *Marine Corps History Division*

strange cantinas at the far ends of the earth; and they spoke fondly of Milwaukee beer. Rifles were high and holy things to them, and they knew five-inch broadside guns. They talked patronizingly of the war, and were concerned about rations. They were the Leathernecks, the Old Timers: collected from ship's guards and shore stations all over the earth to form the 4th Brigade of Marines."

The transport USS *Hancock* arrived on the evening of June 13 and immediately began embarking troops and equipment. "Everything was in confusion," Shepherd recalled, as he led his heavily laden platoon up the gangway. Encumbered with rifles, heavy marching order, and web gear, they struggled to negotiate the narrow, twisting passageways. Equipment caught on bulkhead projections, men tripped on the unfamiliar deck, and tempers grew short. For the unwary, hatch coamings (openings between sections of the ship) offered their own brand of torture. The new men who did not duck collided with the steel and

found themselves flat on their backs, nursing sore heads and bruised egos. The physical exertion and the heat below decks caused them to break out in a sweat, soaking their heavy woolen uniforms and causing even more discomfort. Somehow or other Shepherd got his men safely aboard ship. He heaved a sign of relief, "By God, that was really something, but we did it!"

The dock was a frenzy of activity as the frantic quartermaster struggled to get the ship loaded. Captain R. D. Puryear, commander of the supply company, "was trying to keep track of which holds various supplies and equipment was going in, and trying to keep it properly organized. I finally got the ship loaded and we finally shoved off. Instead of sailing as planned, we found ourselves the next morning in New York harbor." To add insult to injury, the *Hancock* was too slow and another ship, USS *Henderson*, named after the Corps' fifth commandant, Gen. Archibald Henderson, was substituted. The *Henderson* remained at anchor for several days, while a convoy formed up, exemplifying the old military adage, "Hurry up and wait!"

The newly embarked Marines were faced not only with a new environment but also with an entirely new jargon: deck (floor), overhead (ceiling), ladder (stairway), passageway (hallway), head (toilet), galley (kitchen). They learned other navy traditions about whose origins they neither knew nor cared. The youngsters became the subject of harmless, time-honored pranks, played on them by old sea dogs. The very newness of the adventure, going off to war, made it exciting and somehow strangely romantic.

Sergeant Karl McCune was startled when "at twelve noon, without any warning other than a blast of the siren, the *Henderson* put out to sea. About ten miles out was the rest of the fleet, composed of the *DeKalb*, *Finland*, *St. Louis*, and one other transport." The USS *DeKalb*, formally the German auxiliary cruiser *Prinz Eitel Friedrich*, had been interned in the Philadelphia Navy Yard at the start of the war. She had been placed in service so quickly that all notices on the ship were still in German. English translations were printed on cards and posted near the German signs.

The convoy had hardly left port when it was discovered that *Henderson* was a long way from being ready for an Atlantic crossing. Nothing seemed to work. "The drinking fountains wouldn't function;

Over the seas to adventure. Long lines of sea soldiers climb the gangway, burdened in full marching order. They wear their overseas covers instead of the wide-brimmed campaign covers. For most, it would be the first time on a ship, exposure to a totally foreign language—overhead, deck, bulkhead, port, starboard—and *mal de mer*! Note the life rafts lining the rails; the U-boat threat was real. *Marine Corps History Division*

the green crew didn't know how to operate the oil-burning ranges in the galley, there were no gaskets for the hatches, and the steering gear broke," Fritz Wise lamented. Shepherd had to stand watch in the rudder compartment "to hand-steer the ship when the mechanical transmission didn't work."

The weather was good, but even so, many of the newly embarked Marines became victims of *mal de mer*. Carl Brannen moaned, "We were stuffed in like sardines, but I happened to get a hammock hung from the overhead. I got seasick the first day by the time we were out of sight of land down

Marine photographers filming the great event. The Marine Corps Publicity Bureau used the send-off for its recruiting brochures and posters. All the military branches realized the value of publicity in attracting men and women to its ranks. *Marine Corps History Division*

Delaware Bay, and remained sick and miserable the entire thirteen days crossing." The sight of so many landlubbers hanging over the rail gave the old salts an excuse to taunt the "dying" men with visions of pork fat, bacon, and other mouth-watering delicacies. Despite misgivings about surviving, most of the men recovered within a day or two.

Shepherd used the time wisely, organizing his platoon and teaching them the new drill. "Because we were attached to the army, we were ordered to change the drill. Fortunately, having been to VMI [Virginia Military Institute], I was an expert so it was not difficult."

Immediately upon reaching the open ocean, the convoy set a zigzag course for France. At night the ships set blackout conditions, hoping to stay invisible to lurking U-boats. In a letter to his wife, Maj. Edward Ball Cole, 6th Machine Gun Battalion, wrote, "I have never seen it quite so dark as it is in the bowels of a ship with the lights out." It certainly was not a pleasure trip, as Second Lieutenant Worton discovered. "We all had to stand duty up in the foretop, along with six Marine enlisted men as lookouts—four hours at a time. The Marines also manned one of the five-inch batteries." Lieutenant Erskine's men "were sent to different places to report what they saw. They were observers and were given a certain sector to keep their eye on."

Corporal H. B. Field, in *Over the Top*, wrote, "The *Henderson* was one of the escorts and so [we] had to be doubly watchful for subs and hostile craft. After several days out, we received a wireless saying a ship had been torpedoed and was sinking fast." The men were ordered to wear their life jackets at all times. Shepherd was assigned lookout duty and took a turn on a gun crew. "It was a very tense time" because German submarines were on the prowl.

At 10:20 p.m., June 23, a hundred miles off the coast, a sharp-eyed lookout spotted the wake of a German U-boat and sounded the alarm. "A light sea was running, and [the] phosphorescent glow of the whitecaps furnished the means by which the enemy craft were sighted," the *History of the First Battalion, Fifth Regiment* noted. "Two torpedoes flashed their way toward the *DeKalb* [one passed ahead and the other astern], but missed by a narrow margin. Meanwhile, the guns of the transport fired a salvo at the submarines, and at full speed the ship plunged away from the scene of the near disaster." Major Cole happened to be on the stern. "I watched the fall of our aft five-inch battery, and a destroyer dropping depth bombs, which sent up a cloud of spray. It was certainly exciting."

No other U-boats were sighted, and on the morning of June 26, 1917, the *DeKalb* passed through the minefields and pulled into the wel-

The waterfront of St. Nazaire, the first glimpse of France for the Marine Brigade. The French were in awe of these youngsters, with their irrepressible cheerfulness. Their own men were worn down by four bloody years of fighting. The Marines immediately noticed the absence of military-age men—mostly women and children populated the villages.
Marine Corps History Division

coming harbor of St. Nazaire. Their excited passengers lined the rails catching their first glimpse of *La belle France*. One rubbernecker was disappointed. "France did not look anything like I thought it would. I had expected to see everything smart and sort of all dressed up. But here it was old-fashioned. The lighthouses and cottages [were] painted all colors, pink, yellow, and blue; and the people as quaint as the town." His bemused buddy swore up and down, "This place ain't France, I seen too many movies of Paris down

in Tennessee, where I come from." The majority of the men had never been far from home, much less to a foreign country. Everything was new and exciting for the brash, high-spirited youngsters. They were here to beat the "Dutchmen" (Germans) and save the French.

Henderson with the remainder of the 5th Marines arrived the next day. The regimental commander, Col. Charles A. Doyen, reported for duty to the 1st Division (Regular), American Expeditionary Force. The troops stayed on the ships for

Waiting for everyone to debark—and the full marching order gets very heavy. Note the Marine field music with the bugle (near the middle, smoking a cigarette). Many orders were passed by this method, including assembly, chow call, taps, officers call, and reveille, —dozens of separate calls. *Marine Corps History Division*

The small French boxcars were built to transport forty men or eight horses—thus the nickname "40 & 8." They did not have a suspension system and were very uncomfortable. It wasn't too bad close to the door where Marines could watch the scenery and get fresh air. *Marine Corps History Division*

several days waiting for orders. Second Lieutenant Worton explained the delay. "Those of us who served in France were no longer naval troops. We were attached to the army for duty and came under their regulations. Even our muster roles were sent to the adjutant general of the United States Army and not the Commandant of the Marine Corps. It took the army some time to figure this out and send us orders."

Doyen was dismayed to learn that his regiment was not going to be kept intact. Major Wise lamented, "We were pretty badly split up . . . one battalion in St. Nazaire, half a battalion in England, and my battalion a few miles from Menaucourt."

Captain David Bellamy exclaimed, " 'First to fight' has been changed to 'First to work!' " Marines found themselves on working parties, as guards and the most hated assignment of all, cops (military police)—but they did their duty, much to the dismay of the locals.

Second Lieutenant W. B. Jackson overheard a black American stevedore plaintively complain,

Organization of the Marine Brigade

Fifth Regiment (Neville)
First Battalion (Turrill): 17th, 49th, 66th, and 67th Companies
Second Battalion (Wise): 18th, 43rd, 51st, and 55th Companies
Third Battalion (Berry): 16th, 20th, 45th, and 47th Companies
8th Machine Gun Company, Supply Company, and Headquarters Company

Sixth Regiment (Catlin)
First Battalion (Shearer): 74th, 75th, 76th, and 95th Companies
Second Battalion (Holcomb): 78th, 79th, 80th, and 96th Companies
Third Battalion (Sibley): 82nd, 83rd, 84th, and 97th Companies
73rd Machine Gun Company, Supply Company, and Headquarters Company

Sixth Machine Gun Battalion (Cole)
15th Company, 77th Company, 23rd Company, and 81st Company

Crowds lined the overpasses to watch *les Americains*. "Ah, it's great to be young, immortal, and a hero to the local citizens." *Marine Corps History Division*

"My pleasure, sir, I like being up to my butt in mud and water." Duckboard pathways were so narrow that one person had to give way to the other—and often it boiled down to which man was senior. *Morgan Dennis,* Dear Folks at Home

"The jack tars (seamen) they is all right—and the army boys they is all right too, but them guys with a 'world and a buzzard' [Marine emblem] on their hats, they ain't human." The 2nd Battalion, 5th Marines, (Wise) was lucky; they received orders to go to the training area at Gondrecourt by train, the famous "40 & 8," derived from the stencil on the boxcars.

Corporal Paradis was not happy. "We were jammed into those famous 40 *hommes* and 8 *cheveaux* boxcars, which meant 40 men or 8 horses. As I remembered it, they had a recent load of horses because the car smelled like a horse barn." They were unlike anything the men had ever seen before. Light and flimsy, the boxcars were about fourteen feet long and equipped with a diabolical arrangement of heavy plank seats along the sides, which were convenient during the day, but made

it absolutely impossible to get any sleep at night. There was not a spot in the car where a man could stretch out flat. The cars did not have air brakes; just large discs the size of dinner plates, which clashed loudly together when the cars bumped.

Doyen soon learned that his Marines were "odd man out"; the 1st Division already had four infantry regiments, its full complement. Victor F. Bleasdale explained, "We shared in the organization of a new division—the Second Division—with two regiments of Marines and two Army regiments—the so-called square division." The Marine Brigade, as it was called, consisted of the 5th Regiment, 6th Regiment, still in the United States awaiting transportation, and the 6th Machine Gun Battalion formed the 2nd Division's 4th Brigade.

The Army's 9th and 23rd infantry regiments, three artillery battalions (12th, 15th, and 17th), and the 2nd Engineer Regiment completed the 2nd Division's table of organization. At full strength, the division contained more than 28,000 soldiers and Marines. The Marine Brigade numbered 280 officers and 9,164 men, the largest tactical unit the Corps had ever fielded up to that date.

After a day's travel, the battalion detrained at the small village of Menaucourt, where it was welcomed by bouquet-laden children, happily shouting, "*Soyez les bienvenus!* (welcome)." Half the men were billeted in old leaky French barracks and the rest in various farm buildings. Almost every building had its steaming stack of manure piled high to the right or left of the front door. Surface drainage from these stacks moved thickly in shallow ditches, on both sides of the unpaved streets. Human excrement was disposed of in soakage pits of the privy type except when homes bordered the town creek. Then the privy houses straddled the creek, providing "running water."

Major Robert Denig described his experience: "The whole [barracks] floor is muddy and in one place it's six inches deep. Water is brought in by wagon and is treated with a chemical that makes you sick. Hot water can't be had. To take a bath you stand on your trunk and have someone swab you down in ice-cold water. I am covered from head to toe with thick sticky mud that dries as hard as brick. There are narrow wooden walkways, called 'duck walks,' throughout the camp. They are very slippery and hard to negotiate, especially when two people meet—one has to give way and that usually means stepping into the knee deep mud." Private Alfred Schiani lucked out. "My platoon was assigned to the upper part of a barn . . . a gold mine; it was the storage place for cognac."

Schiani's platoon wasn't the only outfit that found a cognac mine. "There was plenty of liquor for our men," Bill Worton mentioned casually. "They'd go through French villages and they could pick up all the brandy they wanted, any time. There was this feeling—if they wanted brandy, let them have it, nobody gave a damn . . . and nobody could have stopped it . . . why, hell, these French farmers would be out giving those kids a bottle of wine and biscuits and cheese."

Don Paradis found a "tot" of rum a godsend on a cold night. "Our canteens were filled with chicory coffee, spiked with rum. I shall never forget the warm glow that you felt in your stomach when that hot rum coffee hit bottom."

Under instructions of the Chasseurs Alpins, the Blue Devils, Marines learn to string barbed wire. The French veterans had learned the hard way that such barricades were essential to break up enemy attacks—but they needed constant repair while under enemy fire. Repairs were made at night and were extremely dangerous. Belts of wire many yards thick were constructed in front of the trenches. *Marine Corps History Division*

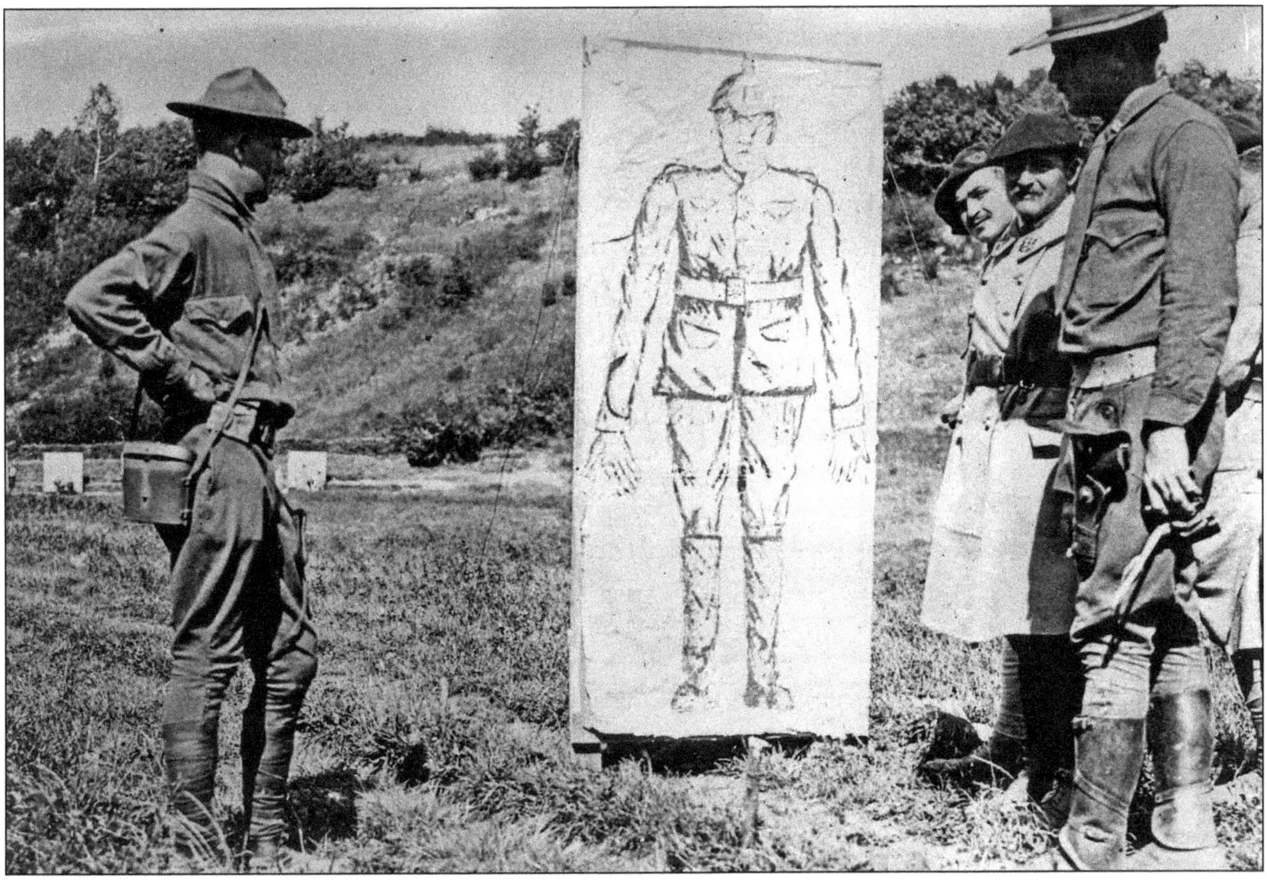

Marine officers and French tutors scrutinize a German silhouette target. The officer on the right has a .45-caliber pistol in a left-handed holster. By the looks on their faces, the shooter must have been in the "black." *Marine Corps History Division*

Blue Devils and Marines training to use signaling devices, semaphore (signal flags), and signal lamps. *Marine Corps History Division*

The veteran 115th French Chasseurs Alpins, known as the "Blue Devils," was paired up with Wise's battalion for training in trench warfare. Second Lieutenant Shepherd was impressed with its commander as he shouted passionately in French, *"En avant, tourjours en avant,"* and then repeated the phrase in heavily accented English, "Forward, always forward." The French soldier's fierce declaration struck a responsive cord with the young officer: "The Chasseurs had fighting spirit!" The Blue Devils earned their nickname from a dark blue uniform and beret; the beret carried a distinctive French horn insignia. They considered themselves a *corps d'elite* and were very proud of their war record. Shepherd was grateful for the instruction. "None of us had any combat training. All we knew

The French instructors tried to pass on their conception of élan, however, they soon found the Americans were more than game to mix it up with the Germans. Bayonet training was thought to impart a more aggressive spirit—especially with lifelike dummies that one could shove an eighteen-inch bayonet through. *Marine Corps History Division*

Shooting the .45-caliber automatic under the watchful eyes of French instructors. The shooter in the foreground is experienced, as noted by his relaxed stance and the way he is holding the weapon. He appears to be an NCO—has had years of practice—and does not need further instruction. *Marine Corps History Division*

were squads left, squads right, and extended order formations. The Landing Force Manual was our only textbook."

The Blue Devils spent the entire summer training the Marines. They paired one of their companies with an American counterpart. Fritz Wise related that "right after breakfast we marched out to the training area, met the French officers, and the day's work began. We dug a series of trenches . . . took up the new method of bayonet fighting . . . [were] showed how to conduct trench raids [and were] put through a gas chamber . . . and given a workout with those damnable French Chauchat automatic rifles. The men looked upon the French instructors as gods, for they knew they were being trained by veteran troops." The French trained the Americans in

Both sides strung miles of barbed-wire obstacles in front of the main line of defense. The maze of wire was designed to slow attackers, as well as to channelize them into pre-sited fields of fire. Artillery was often used to destroy the obstacles and create lanes the infantry could use to close on the frontline trenches. Often the bombardment only succeeded in creating more tangles of wire. *Marine Corps History Division*

Gas training. After donning masks, the Marines enter a sunken bunker where an irritant simulates the more deadly gas. *Marine Corps History Division*

trench warfare, a highly specialized type of operation that evolved after four years of bloody fighting.

Merwin Silverthorn described the trench system: "The troops lived underground in what was called dugouts. Those dugouts had to have a circuitous entrance and exit on account of gas. They were hung with burlap curtains with an air space in between, and then six to eight feet more burlap curtains that were heavily covered with gas neutralizing chemicals. There were three bands of trenches: the frontlines, the support positions, which would be some miles to the rear, and the reserve positions, which would be some miles to the rear of that. They were heavily fortified by two or three bands of barbed wire, each having two or three aprons. The barbed wire was protected by automatic fire and an artillery barrage, which was called a box barrage. It would literally come down 100 meters in front of you and make a wall of steel."

It was at this time that the greenhorns were introduced to the gas mask, one French and one British. Captain Bellamy found that "they are not as smothering as we thought. A rubber mask [goes] over the head, a pair of clippers to clasp the nose and prevent breathing through it, and a mouthpiece to grip in the teeth. You breathe through it and down through a rubber tube that is connected with a tin can of chemicals held in the canvas case held around the neck. The French mask is a wet and smelly thing that is held about the face. Both kinds have goggles affixed." They were instructed

in its use and "practiced, practiced, practiced," until the mask could be put on in five seconds "or the erstwhile Marine would be a corpse." Headquarters published an order that required that "Within two miles from the frontlines, the box respirator and mask must be carried, with the respirator in the 'alert' position."

One Marine said, "[Wearing the mask] reminded me of the stocks used by the New Englanders in the early days to punish offenders. The big, clumsy mask rested on the chest, a few inches below the chin. The gas mask was suspended on the chest by a strap that went around the neck. A string attached to both sides of the carrier ran around the body to keep it from flopping about."

Private Warren R. Jackson described the result of the dreaded shout, "Gas!": "We were to hold our breath and get on the mask in the minimum time, pulling the elastic straps back over the head, inserting the rubber mouthpiece through which a fellow was to try and breathe, adjusting the almost unbearable nosepiece, and feeling the mask to make sure it filled closely about the face and under the chin."

Private Levi E. Hemrick remembered when "the silence of the night was broken by the loud, frightful cry of 'GAS.' The great mass of men was jarred to wide awakeness and instantly hands began reaching for gas masks and a jumping, scrambling, pushing mass of human bodies were trying to wedge their way into that dark narrow aisle."

The threat of gas was a very real one. In the early morning hours of April 13, a German artillery barrage lasting more than four hours struck the 1st Battalion, 6th Marines. Of the estimated 3,000 shells, 1,800 were gas. One mustard-filled 105mm shell struck the wooden sleeping quarters of a sixty-man platoon. The men "all suffered from conjunctivitis, many having infected lungs and several are badly blistered, especially between the legs . . . caused by the premature removal of masks and the failure to promptly evacuate the area."

In one area occupied by the 6th Marines, where five hundred of the mustard gas shells fell, 305 enlisted men and 9 officers had to be evacuated to a hospital area; there were 19 fatalities.

Second Lieutenant Louis B. Jones was one who was evacuated. "The mustard gas would burn a great big blister anyplace where you are accustomed to perspire—under your arms, between

Gas attacks were a very real threat and had to be taken seriously. Here a sign announces a gas alert zone, where the mask had to be carried in the alert position—hanging on the chest, within easy reach. *Marine Corps History Division*

A gas alarm has just been given, and these men are scrambling to put on their masks. Helmets come off, then masks are retrieved from the carrier and quickly placed over the head. The Germans often mixed high-explosive and gas shells—a deadly combination. *Marine Corps History Division*

your legs. I remember a French doctor putting a bicarbonate of soda compress on the family jewels and he forgot to take it off. About four days later it had dried on my skin, so he put his foot on me, gave a big tug, and pulled it off. OUCH!"

Shepherd remembered the training included drill in French—"*Adroit par quatre*" (squad right), "*Avant*" (forward march), and "*Arretez*" (halt)—until the regimental commander found out. "Well, he quickly put a stop to this monkey business." English became the order of the day.

Despite the language difficulties, friendships blossomed, helped along by quantities of vin blanc or vin rouge served in the officer's mess or out of the bottle in the field.

Sergeant Gerald Thomas loathed the training but thought it did prepare them for what lay ahead. "The only place you could drill and train was on areas that were not tillable, which meant that they were really marsh meadows. We were wet every day—the place was icy cold. We worked on bayonet, fired grenades, and we hiked. We'd be

Gas Warfare

Gas was originally used as a physiological weapon meant to instill confusion and panic among the enemy prior to an attack. Tear gas and even sneezing powder were used early in World War I. The introduction of chlorine gas, however, escalated the use of chemicals from a distracting irritant to a deadly weapon. It was first used by the Germans, who released a cloud of chlorine gas on April 22, 1915, against the Allied forces at Ypres. The lethal gas not only created a panic that opened a four-and-one-half-mile gap in the Allied lines, it also caused fifteen thousand casualties. Both sides quickly developed gas masks for protection against the horrible weapon, while at the same time rushed their own weapons of mass destruction into production. Asphyxiants included chlorine, phosgene (which smelled like new-mown hay), and diphosgene. Chlorine, the most common, formed hydrochloric acid when it came in contact with moisture such as that found in the lungs and eyes. It destroyed the respiratory organs, leading to a slow death by asphyxiation.

Mustard gas, a blistering agent, was the most dreaded of all chemical weapons in World War I. It attacked moist skin—eyes, lungs, armpits, and groin. The oily agent produced large burnlike blisters. Mustard gas was long lasting and would hang about in low areas for hours, even days. A Marine jumping into a shell crater could find himself blinded, with skin blistering and lungs bleeding.

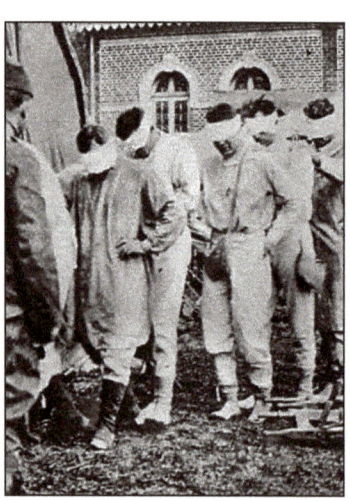

Pitiful lines of gas-blinded Marines head for the hospital ward. Their clothes have been stripped off to rid them of the impregnated mustard gas. Many will regain their sight—others will not be so fortunate. *Marine Corps History Division*

DEVIL DOG AND BLUE DEVIL

Close friendships developed between the battle-hardened Blue Devils and the inexperienced American youngsters. Of course, the process was hurried along by the French proclivity to cement the friendship with a liberal dose of spirits. *Morgan Dennis,* Dear Folks at Home

gone about twenty-four hours and go out and spend the night in the trenches until two o'clock in the morning, and then we'd march back to our camp. We got tough, we stayed tough. When we went to the trenches, we were so damn mean that we would have fought [our] own grandmothers!"

Many of the Marine officers attended special schools. Shepherd was assigned to the "Chef de Section," French platoon commander's school. "Classes started at eight o'clock and go until eleven. Then we'd have a wonderful French lunch (*dejuener*) with wine and often champagne. When the luncheon was over, we'd go over to an old cemetery and sleep among the graves until school started again about two p.m. That was my idea of a good detail."

Second Lieutenant Alfred H. Noble had a different experience and was disappointed with the Army Infantry Specialists School. "We were very much novices," Noble recalled. "We'd had no

Here a squad advances on the run in open field training. This tactic was totally out of date because of the machine gun and masses of barbed wire—as the Marine Brigade would soon learn at Belleau Wood. *Marine Corps History Division*

Major General "Black Jack" Pershing inspecting the 5th Marines. General Pershing is the officer on the extreme left wearing the highly polished riding boots. The dour, strong-minded Pershing was just what America needed to keep the Allies from absorbing them into its own ranks as replacements. *Marine Corps History Division*

experience at all, and all the French officers and men, and the British, were military snobs, as far as we were concerned. They felt we should have been put under their command. And we would have all been under their command if it hadn't been for General Pershing, who held out."

Pershing's chief of staff, Brig. Gen. James G. Harbord and future commander of the Marine Brigade, wrote scathingly of the British and French demand for American troops as fillers for their own depleted ranks. "Our allies [Britain, France]

hate each other but they are in agreement on America as a common resource. It is all a question of how many troops shall go with each. They want all our infantry and machine guns." Pershing held the line according to Harbord. "The commander in chief insisted that our men go into line under their own officers, must be trained according to American standards, and must preserve our national identity. However, if there is a legitimate emergency demanding the use of our divisions, he would put them in."

Flare! Men outside the trenches would freeze, hoping that by remaining motionless, they wouldn't attract fire. Nervous sentries were constantly setting them off. *John W. Thomason Jr., featured in his book* Fix Bayonets!

Chapter 3

A Time in the Trenches

The war was in its fourth year when the American Expeditionary Force reached France. The slaughter had been horrific—Britain and France had been bled dry. Hundreds of thousands of men were gone—an entire generation—and yet the killing continued. After the initial German offensive came a cropper, the contenders went to ground in a line of trenches that extended from the Alps to the North Sea, a distance of more than 450 miles. Military engineers designed an elaborate trench system that defied mere infantry assault.

Shelled remains of the church in Torcy, north of Belleau Wood. Hundreds of destroyed homes and villages littered the countryside as the German juggernaut rolled forward. *Marine Corps History Division*

The abandoned ruins of Bouresches. Thousands of residents fled into an uncertain future, leaving everything behind except what they could carry. *Marine Corps History Division*

The shell of the Belleau school, with Hill 204 in the background. The Germans would take the hill on June 1. It would not be retaken for a month. *Marine Corps History Division*

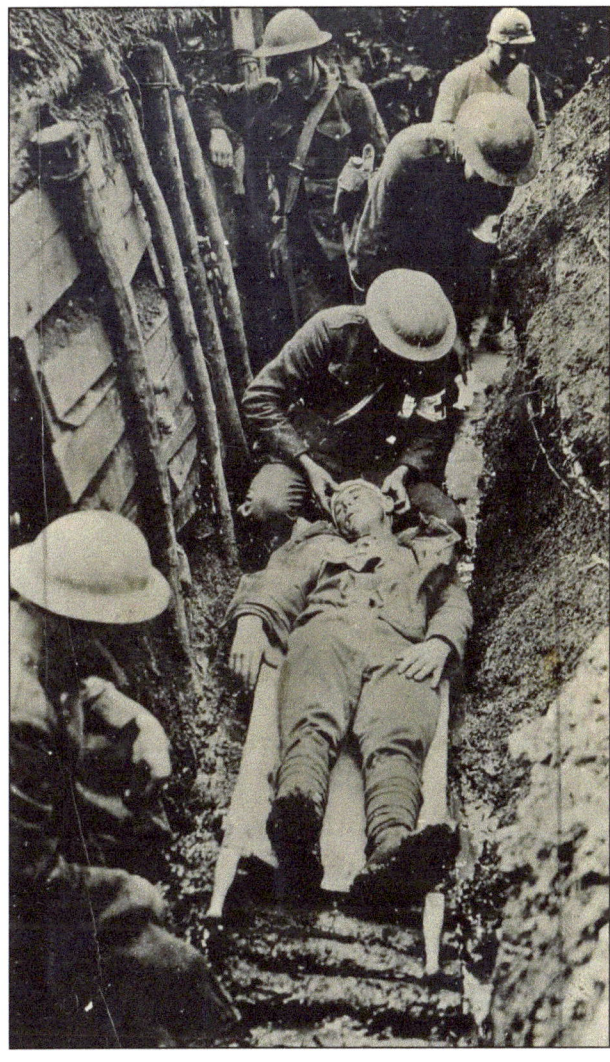

Generally, the system consisted of three parallel trenches. The forward trench looked out into no-man's-land, the unoccupied ground between the two sides. Sentries cautiously peered out into this desolate, forlorn shell-churned ground. Demolished and half-destroyed houses and villages often dotted the landscape.

No-man's-land varied from sector to sector, ranging from within talking distance to more than a kilometer. Multiple belts of barbed wire, frequently 150 feet or more in depth, lined the ground in front of the trench. The wire was covered by rifles and interlocking bands of machine-gun fire to create a crossfire.

Light artillery, the famous French 75s, was positioned within a mile or so of the frontline. The heavy artillery, the 155mm howitzers and guns, was farther back. Carefully constructed fire plans called for the delivery of standing barrages in front of any threatened point. Patrols going forward of the line could be covered by curtain and box barrages if they ran into trouble.

A support trench behind the frontline served as a secondary defense position, as well as offering additional shelter and protection against shellfire. A third "reserve" trench could be as much as several miles behind the first two. Communication trenches served as protected avenues of approach among the three systems.

Long lines of youngsters headed to the front, full of excitement, and a little anxiety, if the truth be known. A great adventure—and the last one for many of them. *Marine Corps History Division*

The wounded base drum of the 5th Marines. Note the three service stripes and the one wound stripe. The Indian head design over the eagle represents the 2nd Infantry Division. The Croix de Guerre has a palm and star representing three awards for distinguished service. The drum head has been preserved—wound stripe and all— and is currently displayed in the entranceway of Lejeune Hall, Quantico, Virginia. *Marine Corps History Division*

By the spring of 1918, the 4th Marine Brigade was ready to take its place in the trenches, under the instruction of a French brigade. Battalions of the 5th and 6th regiments occupied forward trenches in rotation, both regiments sending one battalion to the frontline and holding two in reserve.

A quiet sector with well-developed defenses was picked out: "the Toulon Sector, on the heights of the Meuse southeast of Verdun," the site of a savage bloodbath in 1916. Word swept through the billets: "We're moving up!" Excited youngsters rolled packs and struggled into equipment. Corporals and sergeants hurried them on with shouts and an occasional prod. Platoon commanders, not much older then the men in ranks—Bill Worton was "a mere boy of twenty"—stood on the sidelines, trying to stay out of the way. Long-service captains knowingly glanced at watches, waiting for the battalion commanders—iron-fisted Fritz Wise, Johnny "The Hard" Hughes, "Hiking Hiram" Bearrs—to appear. Finally, all was ready. Long formations, "arrow straight," lined the narrow village streets. "Leather-lunged" old-timers shouted the command, "Forward march!" and the Marine Brigade stepped off to battle.

The first casualty occurred at a train station a short distance from the frontlines. As the Marines detrained, they were spotted by a German Rumpler

Human remains littered the battlefield. Identification of the corpses was almost impossible due to the advanced state of decay and lack of identifying marks or tags. Two Marines killed in action in the town of Bouresches were not found until two years after the battle—too late to identify them. *Marine Corps History Division*

C.IVC.6715/16 observation plane, which called down long-range artillery fire. The first two rounds were uncomfortably close but did not cause any casualties. The third round came whistling in and landed in the middle of the 5th Regiment's band equipment, causing one casualty. A piece of shrapnel pierced the base drum, earning the instrument the right to wear a wound stripe.

On St. Patrick's Day, the Marine Brigade relieved French battalions in the line. Immediately after dark the heavily burdened columns left the reserve positions. They passed batteries of artillery along the road, dim lights visible here and there, through the remains of a village whose ragged walls looked naked and ghostly against a dark sky-line. They entered a shallow communication trench, in single file, heavy marching order on their backs, rifles slung over shoulders and gas masks at the alert. The trench deepened—up to the waist—cutting right and then left—zigzag—to contain the impact of a lucky shell. Mud-caked shoes made it difficult to walk in the slime. It stuck to uniforms, equipment—and, despite their best efforts, smeared weapons with a claylike muck. A foul stench hung in the air, which many veterans recognized instantly as the cloying stench of long-dead bodies.

The column stopped and started, accordion-like, yet they pressed on. Ladderlike "duck boards" occasionally tripped the unwary or the exhausted, sending them crashing loudly to the bottom of the trench, and bringing down the whispered wrath of an NCO or officer. The inky blackness served to bring about a feeling of isolation, heightening fear and loneliness. They fought off weariness, afraid

German Reconnaissance Planes

The *Flieger Abteilung* (flying section) was the primary air reconnaissance organization for the German army. It was composed of specialized aircraft that were designed for intelligence gathering. One, the two-seater Albatros C.VII, performed low-level frontline observation duties. Marine Albert Campbell swore that "the aircraft pilots could even tell where men had traveled by simply looking at the paths that had been made in the fields of grain and wet grasses." Vic Bleasdale had a chance to get even. "Anyone acquainted with the mechanics of shooting a wild duck knows that shooting an airplane down is just like taking candy from a baby. This German plane came around and I just riddled that son-of-a-bitch with bullets."

Another, the German Rumpler C.IV, with its twenty-one-thousand-foot ceiling, was one of the world's first high-altitude spy planes. It was used for long-range reconnaissance photographic missions deep behind enemy lines. It proved remarkably adept at bringing its two-man crew back safely with important information on the Allies' backyard. However, on June 17, 1918, German pilot Otto Roosen received a rude awakening. "An Allied pilot came from above, out of the sun. It happened so fast that I never knew what happened. All of a sudden zip-bang! Bullets all around me. My engine stopped and my observer was killed. I crash landed, flipping the Rumpler over on its back. My legs were scalded by hot water, but at least I was alive."

to fall asleep and be left behind. Except for a few officers, no one knew where they were headed. There was no stopping; they had to be in position before daylight. Suddenly a flare blossomed. The men froze as they had been taught—sudden movement attracts the "eye" of an alert observer—and held their breath. Had they been spotted? The column moved out—lucky this time, just a nervous sentry—and entered a deeper portion of the trench, the frontline, with its fire step and living dugouts.

Nervous sentries set off flares to turn night into day. In the sudden light, enemy soldiers turned into bushes and shrubs. However, folds in the ground, shell holes, shrubbery, and dim light often concealed danger. Trench raids were a constant threat, as both sides sent out patrols to snatch prisoners for intelligence purposes. *John W. Thomason Jr.,* Fix Bayonets!

Rats, hateful creatures that haunted the trenches and dugouts. Bold and almost fearless, they fed on the dead. *Morgan Dennis,* Dear Folks at Home

Guides directed the exhausted men to dugouts. They entered the underground shelter by a circuitous entranceway that was hung with burlap curtains that were impregnated with a gas neutralizing agent. Merwin Silverthorn described the living conditions. "You lived in utter darkness, unless you had a candle, and even then it only cast a dim shadow. You slept on some type of frame that had chicken wire that you laid your blanket on. There was no mattress, just your blanket. The dugout was infested with rats—huge rats, not field mice."

Sergeant Daniel E. Morgan shot the loathsome things. "Down in the dugout, where we slept, it was partly filled with water, so we built our bunk up on the wall, and many a night I sat there by the candle, shooting rats and watching them fall into the water. After they were shot they laid there and rotted, and oh, how they did smell. The air down there—I have never experienced such foul air."

Despite the terrible conditions, humor kept spirits up. Paradis wrote, "The trenches had water ankle deep and the lower bunks of our dugouts were just out of the water. There were not enough rubber boots for all, and Eddie O'Brien, our company wit, was on duty, standing on the firing step, above the water line, when the corporal came sloshing up the trench to his position. Eddie said, 'Hey, cut out riling the water, don't you know we have to sleep in it tonight?' "

Above: A first sergeant receives the mail for his men in front of the company dugout. The position is solidly constructed and seems to have been built into a boundary fence, using the rock to build up the roof. Note the alert position of his gas mask and the fact that the mailman is not similarly prepared, which will probably be brought to his attention. *Marine Corps History Division*

Right: Beautifully constructed trench, featuring a dry walkway and new supports to keep the dirt wall from caving in. Sandbags seem relatively new and in good shape—a home away from home. *Marine Corps History Division*

Warren Jackson was lucky; he was assigned a dugout recently vacated by the French. "We came to a dimly lighted opening at the left of the trench. A steep flight of stairs led to what appeared to be a room below. And forty feet down was an oblong room, running parallel to the trench above. The place was roughly boxcar shaped. With a low ceiling, the room was about four feet wide

A two-man combat patrol in no-man's-land. Night after night hundreds of men from both sides actively patrolled the area between the two armies. Clashes were usually deadly close-range encounters—bayonets, knives, grenades—with the fallen often left behind in the brutal engagement. *John W. Thomason Jr., Fix Bayonets!*

by fifty to sixty feet long. Running the length of the room, and on the side opposite where we entered, was a double-tiered row of bunks nailed to the floor and wall." The dugout was a classic example of the lengths men went to make a quiet sector comfortable.

The Americans did not understand the concept of a quiet sector and immediately went on the offensive, much to the chagrin of the war-weary French. Bobby Erskine did not think much of the French soldiers. "I thought the French troops were whipped, I didn't think their discipline was very good from what I could see."

Marine Second Lieutenant William Worton learned they had more of a "live and let live" philosophy:

The first raid I went on with a lieutenant in the French army and we were sent over to get a German prisoner. We crawled across no-man's-land and surrounded a lone German. One of the Frenchmen hit him on the head, knocking him out, and we carried him back toward our lines. On the way back, we stumbled onto a German patrol going the

other way. I pulled my pistol—after all, these bastards were there to kill me, I thought. And this Frenchman grabbed me and whispered, "Don't shoot."

"What the hell, they're Germans," I softly replied, not understanding what was going on.

"Sure," he responded, "but they've been over catching a Frenchman; we've been over to get a German. We got our German, they may have their Frenchman, but don't start a row, we'll all get killed. You Americans haven't been in this war long enough to understand."

The Marines did not understand this attitude. They came to France to kill Germans—referred to by the derogatory French slang *Boche*—and end the war: "The more Boche we kill, the quicker the end." An exasperated French general exclaimed, "They [Americans] were irrepressible! They climbed like cats into the highest trees 'to kill the Boche' . . . and began to fire on the enemy sentries or on the [German] platoons running between the first and second line trenches."

Private Wayne W. French was a little more circumspect. His convoy passed a cemetery. "Here's a quiet sector," he remarked to his squad mates. "Let's take over here."

A Lewis machine-gun team using a tree as a platform. Veterans would laugh at their carelessness and inexperience. The team makes a great target for German counterfire and has absolutely no protection from shrapnel. *Marine Corps History Division*

Buddies pay tribute to a fallen comrade. Only two of the graves have identified remains. Identification was often difficult because of the nature of the combat: explosives dismembered the remains and the dead were often lost in the heavy vegetation. *Marine Corps History Division*

The veterans, tongue-in-cheek, boasted that life in the line was mind-numbing monotony broken up by short periods of stark raving terror. The first Marine killed in action was Pvt. Emil Henry Gehrke, 82nd Company, 6th Regiment, on April 1. He was behind the lines on a three-man working party when a German shell landed in their midst. Shrapnel pierced Gehrke's chest, killing him instantly. The other two were wounded, one critically. Gehrke was buried with full military honors, and "his grave was marked with a wooden cross on which there was a square piece of tin bearing his name, number of company, battalion, regiment, nationality, and date of death." Not all Marines received a hero's funeral. Dozens perished and were buried in unmarked graves on the field of battle.

The quiet sector that the Americans took over soon heated up—shooting begat shooting, patrols begat patrols—tit for tat.

April 6: The Germans attempted a raid on the 74th Company in the town of Tresauvaux.

They were repulsed, leaving four dead behind. The Marines lost one man killed and three wounded.

April 17: A mixed force of Marines and French soldiers successfully launched a raid near the town of Demi-Lune. Two Marines were awarded the Croix de Guerre for the action.

April 21: Between 0400 and 0500 in the morning, the Germans shelled the 45th Company and a raiding party launched an assault. It was repulsed before it reached the second wire. The Germans left two officers and one noncommissioned officer killed. The Marine company had three killed and eleven wounded.

Sergeant Gerry Thomas' platoon commander "volunteered" him for the "suicide squad," a hand-picked squad of scouts and observers. "We laid a patrol to move out from a little destroyed village to counter a German effort to mount a raid against us. The Germans realized there was a new outfit in front of them and wanted to get some prisoners to identify us. About midnight we passed through a gap in our wire. We were just starting to fan out when—ZINGO!—we crashed into a big German patrol. Both of us backed off, started shooting, and called for defensive barrages that we had planned before. We fired Very pistols, as a signal to fire the barrage. Our lieutenant got cut off, we had several men wounded, and one man killed. We had a real rough night!"

Major Robert Denig went forward to check the lines. "The trenches were shallow and they had not been able to put our wire, due to the Germans, who did not hesitate to shoot at the slightest movement. We crawled out to a shallow trench caved in

Colonel Victor Bleasdale wearing the French *Fourragère*, which was awarded after being cited three times by the French army. Bleasdale was also awarded the Distinguished Service Cross. His brother was also honored with the same decoration. *Marine Corps History Division*

An injured man is carried to the aid station by his buddy. Navy hospital men were assigned to the Marines at the company, battalion, and regimental levels. These men of mercy were well respected by their Leatherneck comrades, who knew the sailors would risk life and limb for them. *Marine Corps History Division*

by shellfire, to a point blocked by sandbags and old snarled wire. It was moonlight night, so I could see no-man's-land well, just to the German trenches at this point one hundred yards off. In front of us, they had an outpost not forty yards distant. When it gets dark, both sides send out patrols to control the narrow strip. Four days ago the Boche raided the part I was in and killed four, wounded seven, captured one officer and seven enlisted men."

The Marine with the gas mask has just come back from one of the never-ending working parties— dirt-smeared face, mud on boots, ripped trousers. The other clean-shaven Marines are counting their good fortune to have missed the detail. Note the mud-caked trench bottom and the height of the trench— no chance for a sniper to pick off the unwary. *Marine Corps History Division*

Trench Raid

The irrepressible Vic Bleasdale describes a bit of derring-do: "I'm going to attack that goddamn position over there and I'm just going to riddle the son-of-a-bitching place and kill everybody in sight. So I called for volunteers . . . geez, everybody volunteered—everybody in my platoon. So I made an attack across this two hundred yards of field . . . covered by machine guns on either flank. We were lucky, there were a couple of [German machine] guns right in front of us but our guns had riddled them. One son-of-a-bitch was lying in back of his gun with blood pouring out of a dozen holes. A couple of other dead or dying men were lying in front of a bunker entrance. I pulled out a grenade and threw it into the dugout. I pulled my head back, thinking I would dive in right after the explosion—it takes even brave men to recover from its effects—and Jesus Christ, debris came flying right by my face! I dove down into the dugout before anyone could recover. There was a great big German lying on the floor with a beautiful pair of field glasses on his chest. I yanked them off this big Dutchman and dove back out the entrance. Damn, one of my men had a grenade ready to throw. . . . Another split second and he would have thrown it in. 'God, Lieutenant,' he said, 'another second and I would have killed you.' That was enough. I shouted to my men to pull back. We ran across the field and got back without losing a man."

Brigadier General James G. Harbord wearing a French helmet. Harbord had been Pershing's chief of staff and had only recently been promoted. Despite being a U.S. Army officer, he was immediately accepted by the Marines, who gave him unqualified support. He proudly wore the insignia of a Marine—an eagle, globe, and anchor. *Marine Corps History Division*

The Marines settled into a routine of raids, night patrols, artillery barrages, constant working parties, lice, and rats, which infested the dugouts and trenches. For many, the spirit of adventure died in the frontline trenches. The war took on a new dimension—to get it over as soon as possible while struggling to survive. In early May, after fifty-three days in the line, the Marine Brigade was relieved and rejoined the 2nd Division for final training. The brief period in the quiet sector cost 128 Marines killed in action and 744 wounded. Also in May, Brig. Gen. James G. Harbord, U.S. Army, assumed command after his predecessor, Brig. Gen. Charles Doyen, was found physically unfit for duty in the field. Pershing, never known for praising the Marines, told him, "Young man, I'm giving you the best brigade in France—if anything goes wrong, I'll know whom to blame."

The last days of May brought welcome relief for the men of the Marine Brigade. Warm weather had finally arrived, giving them an opportunity to shed their long winter underwear and dry out after an onerous tour of duty in the trenches. They also got a welcome surprise, a rare day off to celebrate Decoration Day, May 30. There were no drills, and at the noon formation, the regimental bands played "Departed Days." For most it was a time of rest and relaxation, a time to write letters, catch up on sleep, or for a lucky few, a date with a local *jeune fille*. Lem Shepherd was one of the lucky ones. He had met "an attractive French girl" and had been invited to dinner. "Naturally, I was all excited about this. [She] was the prettiest mam'selle I'd seen in France. I took the morning primping—I was going to look like a real Marine officer when I arrived for that young lady." Fielding Robinson, his former VMI classmate, was out riding horseback with his new boss, Brigadier General Harbord. Sergeant Gerald Thomas was stuffing himself with food at the regimental galley after listening to the chaplain deliver a gloomy sermon on the "ultimate sacrifice." Acerbic Fritz Wise was in Paris on a three-day pass with his wife, a hospital volunteer. Floyd Gibbons, the flamboyant *Chicago Tribune* correspondent, was also in the city, trying to confirm a rumor that a huge German offensive was bearing down on the "City of Lights."

On 0300 May 27, a massive German offensive smashed through the French and British lines, unnerving the British and French high command. Lem Shepherd explained, "The Germans made a salient that ran down to the Marne River, and that was a straight dash into Paris. All they had to do was go another twenty-five miles!" The attack seemed unstoppable. "Christ, another twenty-four hours and France would be out of the war. That's how close they were to defeat." There were not enough reserves to plug the gap. A hurried call went out to the inexperienced American 2nd Division: "March to the sound of the guns." A French general worried that *les Americains* could not hold and said as much to Col. Preston Brown, the 2nd Division chief of staff. The sharp-tongued Brown indignantly replied, "General, these are American regulars. In a hundred and fifty years they have never been beaten. They will hold."

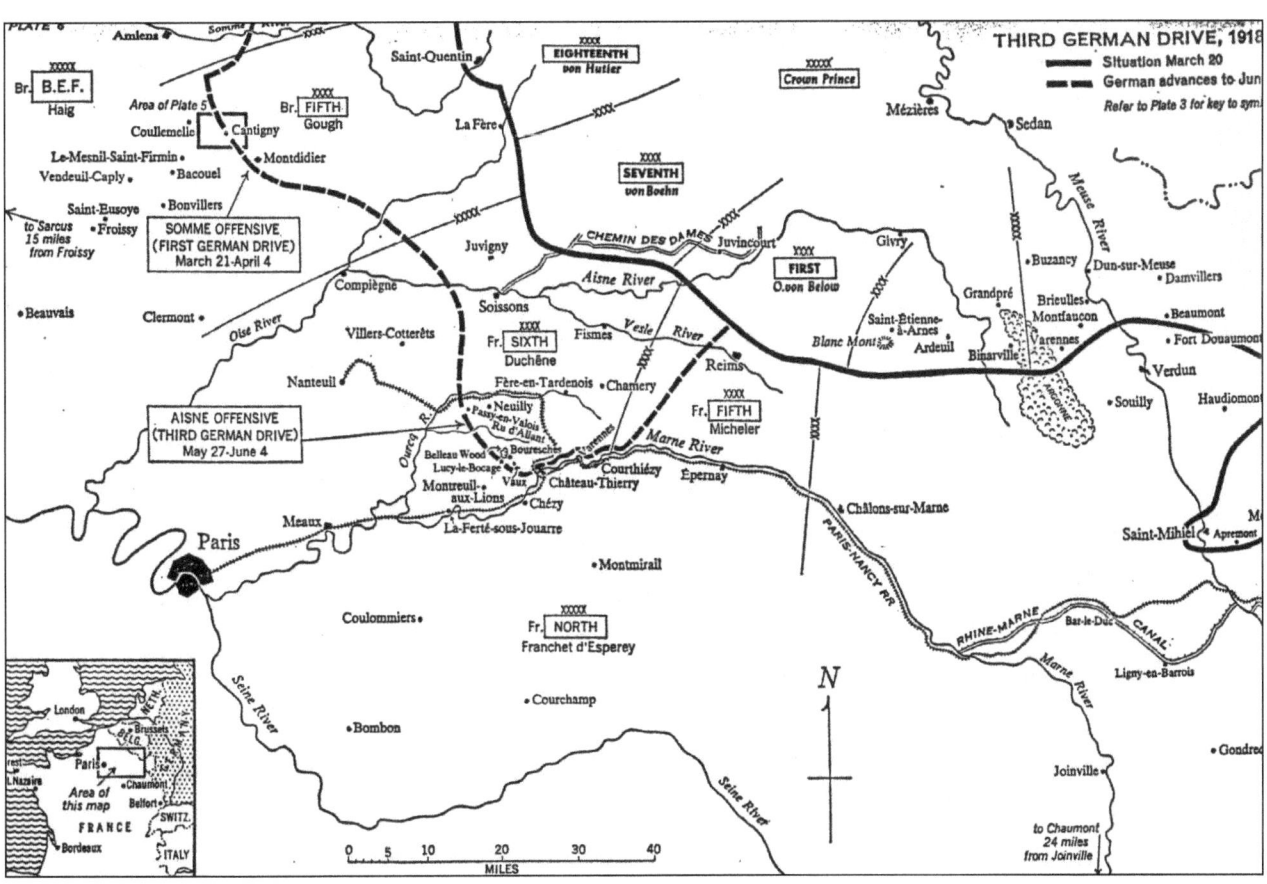

The German attack punched through the weak French frontline positions and threatened Paris, the City of Lights. The French high command was desperate and begged Pershing to use the 2nd Infantry Division to halt the German drive. The situation was so desperate that Pershing gave in. *Northwest of Chateau Thierry: 1 June–10 July (unpublished 2nd Division report)*

German infantry under fire as they move through a wheat field. *Harvey Dunn–National Museum of the Marine Corps*

Chapter 4

The Blooding

The rapid German push toward Paris, coupled with the French troops' weariness, made the immediate deployment of the 4th Brigade a necessity.

Major Wise and his wife were at a friend's home when the telephone rang. "My adjutant, Lt. James Hennen Legendre, told me, 'We've been ordered up to the front at once.' I'll be there, I told him." Harbord and Robinson had just finished their ride when "A sergeant hurried toward us with news of orders to move . . . packing started at a furious pace." Shepherd

"Fall in!" One of the 250-man companies in formation in front of their billets. The war-weary French were amazed at the youthfulness and physiques of *les Americain*. *Marine Corps History Division*

got the word just as he was climbing on a bicycle to go to dinner. "I was told to turn out my platoon and stand by for boarding *camions*. I knew this meant action, otherwise we would have moved by foot. All I could do was send my orderly with a note of apology to my *Marianne*." A messenger found Thomas and told him to report to his platoon commander. "When I reported to Lt. David Redford, a hard-bitten little fellow from Rhode Island, he told me to make sure the men drew ammunition and rations. We were moving out, but he didn't know where."

Wise hitched a ride in an ambulance and got back just in the nick of time. "The bugle sounded assembly and the battalion fell in on the road, alongside the *camions*. Platoon leaders' whistles blew and the men climbed aboard." Second Lieutenant W. B. Jackson, 6th Machine Gun Battalion, wrote in his memoirs, "In the early morning hours the *camions* arrived and we embarked. Nobody seemed to have any idea where we were heading or why. The *camions* were driven by Annamite drivers, two to a truck, small weary heathen in khaki and crested helmets."

Camions were French army trucks that were notorious for being uncomfortable. They held twenty to twenty-five men who sat on narrow wooden seats along each side and another in the middle. The wheels were solid rubber, which jostled the men mercilessly on the pothole-filled roads. Long funnels of suffocating dust engulfed the convoys, adding to their misery. At times, the *camions* sped along with reckless abandon, scaring the hell out of their passengers. First Lieutenant Chester H. Fraser of the 18th Company noted, "Lucky if we don't get killed before reaching the front."

The massive fourteen-mile convoy carrying the 2nd Division, twenty-eight thousand men and seven thousand horses, skirted Paris and haltingly made its way toward the town of Meux in central France. "The weather was clear, and the sun hot and merciless. . . . The hard Rue Nationale and the lesser roads bore a top-dressing of dust, as fine and white as talcum powder." Second Lieutenant E. D. Cooke grumbled, "It billowed in long funnels from the tail of each section. Clouds of grit swirled in through both ends of our truck, and with each jounce of the springs, small geysers of dirt squirted

Marines in full marching order board *camions* for the one-hundred-mile trip to Chateau-Thierry. *Marine Corps History Division*

Thirty or so Marines were packed into the uncomfortable *camions*, which were driven by Annamites or Tankanese from French Indochina. The drivers had been at their wheels for seventy-two hours and had the habit of falling asleep. *Marine Corps History Division*

End of the line. Marines debark and move forward. Officers are mounted on horses in the background. *Marine Corps History Division*

French horsedrawn artillery pulling back from the front through a village that has yet to experience war. Hundreds of thousands of horses and mules were used during the war. Mechanized vehicles were still in their infancy. The guns appear to be the famous French 75s, which caused the Germans so much trouble. *Marine Corps History Division*

up at us from between the floorboards. Some of the men tried wearing their gas masks, but decided that air with dirt was better than no air at all, so took them off."

Sergeant Gerald Thomas said, "[We] would go awhile and stop, and then go a little while. We stopped where there was a little rise in the road. I looked over there, and it was like Napoleon at the Battle of Austerlitz. Marshall Foch surrounded by a group of staff officers was watching us riding by. I knew damn well who it was because I had seen his picture."

General Harbord recalled, "Sometimes it seemed difficult to gain a foot of distance. Trains, trucks, wagon, civilian, and farm vehicles of every description, all headed from the front, would congest and block the road sometimes for half an hour at a time so that movement forward was impossible." The massive tide of humanity played havoc with the American transportation schedules. Some units were delayed for hours, others had to start the move by shank's mare.

It was the first time Marines had seen the human cost of war. Private Levi E. Hemrick wrote, "On the side of the road were sick, wounded, and deadly tired soldiers, old tottering men and women. Almost every one of them were loaded down to and beyond their capacity to carry their most pre-cious possessions saved from their deserted homes. Some had their goods tied to the frames of old bicycles and were pushing them along. The most fortunate had their household goods lashed on two-wheel carts, most of them pulled by a horse, and some by manual labor. One old man was seen pushing a farm wheelbarrow before him on which was sitting a feeble old lady. There were children, and some young mothers with babies in their arms, and others in a family way. Some of the children and babies were sick. One baby had died and the mother was beside the road weeping over the body of her lost child. There were dead horses and two-wheeled carts with both wheels smashed beyond repair."

Late on the afternoon of June 1, the lead elements of the brigade reached its destination on the Paris–Metz road, nine miles north and west of Chateau-Thierry. A signpost pointed to the right— Paris 65 Kilometers. The travel-worn, hungry men disembarked and stood waiting for orders. The outspoken Victor Bleasdale, 15th [Machine Gun] Company, noted, "Between the time we stopped our truck and got off the goddamn things, the Germans had advanced from artillery sound to machine-gun sound. They were coming, boy, they were moving fast toward Paris!" A visibly upset Fritz Wise stood on the side of the road arguing

Above: On the road, "Take ten, smoke if you've got 'em" was the oft-heard shout from NCOs on the march. *Marine Corps History Division*

Left: Hike for fifty minutes out of every hour and rest for ten—hour after hour, toting sixty pounds of weapons and equipment. *Marine Corps History Division*

with a French staff officer, who was trying to convince the short-tempered battalion commander to fall back. Wise shook him off with a gruff retort. "I have come to fight Germans and this is where I intend to do it—and that is that, by God!"

Shortly before noon, Col. Wendell C. "Buck" Neville, regimental commander 5th Marines, roared up in a staff car and singled out Fritz Wise. Neville motioned him over and spread a map out on the hood of the car. Wise peered over his shoulder as the regimental commander traced a line with his finger. He pointed out a spot about one and a half kilometers north of their current position and ordered Wise to form a defensive line

from the northeast corner of Veuilly Wood to a point east and south of Les Mares Farm. "You've got to get there right away. We don't expect the French to stick, and if you don't hurry up, the Germans will get there before we do. And when you get there, you stick! Never mind how many French come through you."

Wise asked, "Who'll be supporting my flanks?"

Neville replied, "I'll let you know as soon as I know myself." Buck climbed back in his car and roared off. Wise ordered the battalion buglers to sound assembly.

Wise was told to tie in with the U.S. 23rd Infantry on the left and the 6th Marines on the

Above: A platoon of Marines waits for "the word." *Marine Corps History Division*

Right: "Hurry up and wait," the age-old tradition. Rush to get there, and then wait for orders. *Marine Corps History Division*

Left: Colonel Wendell Cushing "Buck" Neville, forty-seven-year-old commander of the 5th Marines at Belleau Wood. He was awarded the Medal of Honor for "conspicuous courage, coolness, unaffected bravery under fire" at Vera Cruz in 1914. In 1929 he became the fourteenth commandant of the Marine Corps. *Marine Corps History Division*

right, but when he moved into position, there was no one there. His one thousand Marines faced the German onslaught alone. Remnants of French units passed through their lines in full retreat. *"Retournez, retournez, La guerre est finie,"* they cried, *"La Boche est victorieuse!"* ("Turn back, turn back, the war is over. The Germans are victorious!") The frontline French soldiers—known as *poilus*, a colloquialism which literally translates as "hairy ones"—staggered from fatigue, their ragged uniforms and bloody bandages attested to the hard-fought delaying action. They stared hollow-eyed at the fresh-faced youngsters in the strange field green uniforms.

"They looked fine, coming in there," John Thomason wrote, "Tall fellows, healthy and fit—they looked hard and competent." The French were quiet, too tired to waste energy on needless conversation. It was enough that these strangers were between them and the Germans. One haggard French officer buttonholed Capt. Lloyd "Josh" Williams of the 51st Company. He gestured excitedly toward the rear and, in halting English, ordered the Marine captain to retreat. Williams looked him in the eye and quipped, "Retreat, hell. We just got here!" Williams next sent a cryptic field message to Wise:

To: Battalion Commander, Second Battalion
June 3, 1918, 3:10 P.M.

The French major gave Capt. Corbin written orders to fall back—I have countermanded the order—kindly see that the French do not shorten their artillery range . . .

Lloyd W. Williams
Captain, U.S.M.C.

The battalion moved out, quick time, and less than an hour later reached a narrow road, its designated defense position. From one end to the other, the sector stretched over four kilometers, about two and a half miles. Open ground on their right

French cavalry pass by Marine columns marching to the sound of guns. *Marine Corps History Division*

front gradually sloped upward to a wooded hill (Hill 165) about a half-mile away. Les Mares Farm stood on their left front, while a checkerboard pattern of woods and fields swung away from them on both flanks. The extended frontage forced Wise to place all four companies on line—18th Company on the extreme left, in the northeast corner

The French were in awe of the youngsters in the strange forest green uniforms. *John W. Thomason, Jr., Fix Bayonets!*

Retreat Hell

The famous "Retreat Hell" quip was claimed by many, including Lieutenant Colonel Wise. However, the issue was officially settled by the Marine Corps in 1932, when Lt. Col. Edwin McClellan of the Marine Corps' Marine Corps History Division accepted former Capt. J. D. Murray's explanation (Murray was the battalion second in command). "Captain Corbin, second in command of the 51st [Company], came to me and told me that a French officer had been so insistent with Captain Lloyd Williams that he drop back that he sent Corbin to find out if there were such orders. I told him that there were not and asked him what Captain Williams had said and done. Corbin replied that Williams had tried to explain to the French officer that he couldn't drop back without orders but he became so garrulous that "Josh" finally . . . said impatiently, 'Retreat, hell, we've just gotten here!' McClellan wrote that "there is quite a lot of good information that seems to prove conclusively that Lloyd Williams [made] the statement."

Second Lieutenant Lloyd Williams shortly after being commissioned as a Marine officer on January 8, 1910. Williams was an experienced combat leader when he led his men at Belleau Wood. He had earned his spurs in banana republics after a number of expeditionary landings. Severely wounded and dying, he urged his men to leave him and continue the attack. He was posthumously awarded the Distinguished Service Cross. *Marine Corps History Division*

of the Bois de Veuilly, 43rd Company next in line, 55th Company in and around Les Mares Farm, and the 51st Company on the right flank, south of Hill 142.

Company by company they moved into position, each taking its share of the four-kilometer sector. Captain Lester S. Wass, 18th Company, pushed his men forward. An artillery round exploded in the middle of the column, knocking several down, four never to rise again. The men hesitated, until Wass bellowed, "Get going, what do you think this is, a kid's game?" galvanizing them into action. Captain John Blanchfield and his executive officer, Lem Shepherd, led the 250 men of the 55th Company into a woodline just above the town of Champillon and ordered a halt. The two officers went forward to reconnoiter. As they left the shelter of the trees, a heavy German artillery barrage drove the last French soldiers from the field. Explosions and bursts of flame marked its steady advance over the scarred terrain. The retreating *poilus* withdrew in good order, each group firing a

few rounds before falling back to a new position. They said the Germans were right behind them.

Captain Wass turned to one of his lieutenants, E. D. Cooke, saying, "I would like to see one German, at least." Within minutes an enemy plane swooped down and dropped a string of bombs. Both men dove for cover, but not fast enough for Cooke. A fragment hit him in the derriere, damaging his pride more than his person. "What do I say when people ask where I got hit?" Wass offered several crude suggestions—but it was Cooke's platoon that came up with an appropriate rhyme, which they sang with gusto: "The lieutenant, he

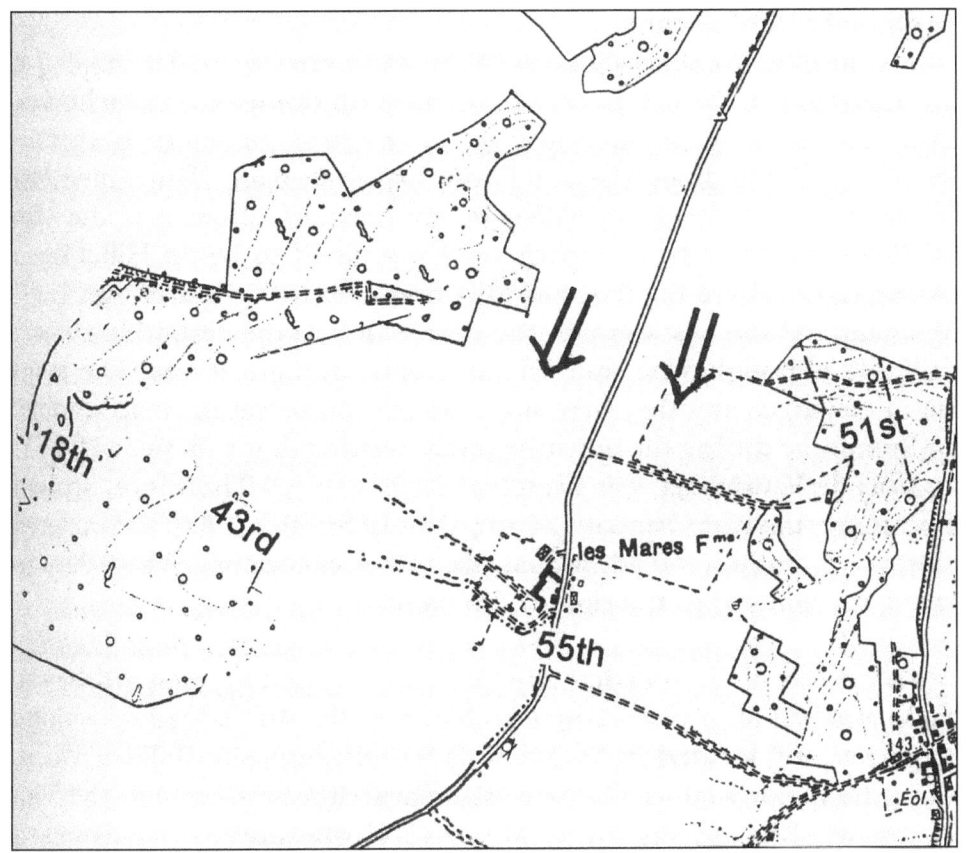

saw an airplane pass, and he caught a piece of shrapnel in the ass."

Blanchfield and Shepherd returned to the shelter of the woods. Shepherd waited impatiently for the order to move forward, but Blanchfield was overwhelmed by the tactical situation. The older man seemed paralyzed with indecision. Finally, he issued a rather vague suggestion, which gave Shepherd the authority to advance the company. Shepherd gathered the four platoon commanders, Lieutenants Tillman, Lineham, Waterhouse, and Lyle, gave them a short brief, and led the company forward "at the double." They formed a skirmish line, the right of the company touching and covering the Champillon–Bussiares road, and its left resting at the Les Mares Farm, using the red-roofed house and barn as part of the defensive position. The farm stood on "rising ground, dotted with clumps of woods, with grain fields here and there, and tall hedges."

German shells reached out, the 88mm "quick-dicks," which hit without warning, and the 77mm "whiz-bangs," with a two-second alert. E. D. Cooke "heard a shell whirring toward me. Then

Les Mares Farm was occupied by the 55th Company under Capt. John Blanchfield, who was killed on the night of June 11. The farm's stone buildings and sturdy fences gave his Marines protection against enemy fire. The open fields surrounding the farm gave the Marines great fields of fire. *Marine Corps History Division*

A *blighty wound*, a British term, was an injury serious enough for evacuation home to Blighty (Britain). The smiling Marine senses that he will soon be away from the hell of combat. *Marine Corps History Division*

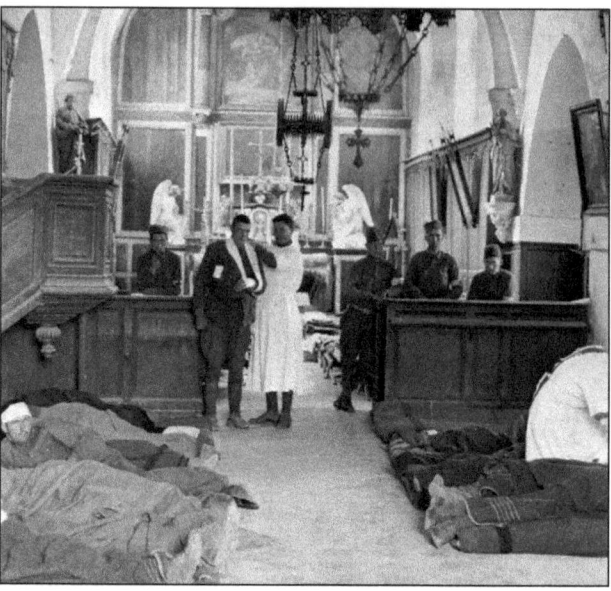

There were so many casualties at Belleau Wood that many public buildings were pressed into service, in this case a church. On June 6 the Marine Brigade suffered more than one thousand casualties. *Marine Corps History Division*

with a final scream of rage the huge piece of ordnance tore itself into a thousand fragments. The air was alive with deadly splinters. They tore at the trees, furrowed the ground, and all too often found a target in human flesh." Cooke was haunted by the plaintive cry of the wounded for a "hospital man." Some were frantic, others pleading, but all were pitiful. Private E. A. Wahl, 6th Marines, heard a scream as a shell exploded. "It landed in a hole where two chaps from another company were lying. Several of us rushed over to the spot and pulled them out. They were horribly cut up, but not dead. A horse tied to a tree about five feet away was killed. I think it was the poor animal that screamed. An ambulance rolled by at that moment and we stopped it, had the boys' wounds dressed, and they were rolled away."

There were no prepared defenses, and there was no time to wait for "proper" entrenching tools. One lieutenant yelled, "Dig for your lives!" Those men who had them broke out small T-handle shovels. Others used anything at hand—bayonets, mess kits, spoons—to dig into the rich farmland. Corporal Glen G. Hill, 76th Company, "took my bayonet and, lying on my side, dug a hole to get myself under cover." Joseph E. Rendinell, 6th Marines, "had to use my hands and bayonet.

Some of the boys wanted to pay a hundred francs or twenty dollars for a shovel. I found a German shovel and dug with that." They dug individual foxholes six or seven feet apart along the company's front. Shepherd described the holes as "little scooped-up hollows similar to a grave but about a foot deep, with earth piled up in front for a parapet," behind a barbed-wire fence. One private wrote, "It's amaing how quickly we dug in, considering we had no shovels. All around me I saw my buddies sinking slowly into the ground, while parapets of soft earth grew steadily up beside them . . . we were grateful that the Heinies hadn't started dropping their nine-inch 'sea bags' on us." All that night they were heavily shelled.

The next morning, Shepherd surveyed their surroundings. "[There was] a little knoll a couple of hundred yards in front of our lines, which I recognized as an important terrain feature. We couldn't include it in our lines because it was a little too far from where we'd been ordered to establish our main line of resistance. I suggested to Blanchfield that we ought to put an outpost out there, because of its good field of fire and observation." Blanchfield concurred. Shepherd led two squads, fourteen men under a sergeant, to the outpost and positioned them with orders to "hold their fire until the enemy was close and then open fire. When the Germans got too close, the men were to withdraw to our lines."

Later in the afternoon, Shepherd grew concerned about the men in the outpost as the German barrage increased, signaling an infantry assault. The outpost was isolated and could get cut off. He went to Blanchfield and requested to check on the small detachment. "Jim, I'm worried about that outpost. I sent them out there and I think I ought to check them." Blanchfield quickly approved. "I must say it was a foolish suggestion," Shepherd recalled, "because they had orders to withdraw but I just wanted to go out there to ensure they did."

A rolling barrage blanketed the Marine positions with deadly shrapnel. Shepherd nodded to his runner, Pfc. Pat Martin, and said casually, "Let's go," belying the fear he felt. Shepherd remembered they had just started out when "a shell landed about ten feet in front of me. I'll always recall it to my dying day. The dirt flew up and I just stood there waiting for the shell to go off. Thank God it was a dud!"

Somehow, the two made it to the outpost just in time to hear the sergeant shout, "Here come the Boches!" The Germans came on in an open formation, scouts to the front, only a few hundred yards away.

A newsman looked at the holes the Marines were digging and nicknamed them "foxholes." Getting below ground often meant the difference between life and death. Unless one took a direct hit, a foxhole provided good protection because shrapnel generally went up and out. *Morgan Dennis,* Dear Folks at Home

The Germans were taken back by the accurate long-range rifle fire. The hours of practice on the rifle range paid off for the Marines as they adjusted their sights to five hundred yards and decimated the enemy ranks. *John W. Thomason Jr.,* Fix Bayonets!

German infantry wore a field gray uniform and a "coal shuttle" helmet, which gave the wearer much more head protection than the flat "tin" helmet of the Americans and British. Note the hand grenade—"potato masher"—hooked on the belt. *Marine Corps History Division*

The outpost was on the forward slope of the knoll where they had good fields of fire. The small group of Marines took the enemy formation under fire with their Springfield .03 rifles. They picked off the enemy scouts and then concentrated on the Germans in the first assault waves. Their accurate rifle fire first surprised, then confused, and finally halted the advance. The Germans set up machine guns in the woods opposite the outpost, and soon a hail of automatic-weapons fire blanketed the knoll. Shepherd took cover behind the brow of the mound, where he could observe the action. "There were several trees on top of the knoll, and I leaned against one of them where I could look over the top and direct the men's fire. All of a sudden something hit me in the neck and spun me completely around. My first thought was, 'My God, a bullet's gone through my gullet!' I was gulping air—funny what you do. I spit in my hand to see if I was spitting blood but I wasn't, so I felt relieved. A bullet cut a groove through my neck and just missed my jugular vein. Another quarter of an inch and I'd be dead."

Despite the heavy enemy fire, Shepherd's small detachment held the position until dark. When the Germans started encircling the position, Shepherd pulled the men out safely, bringing out two wounded. Shepherd accompanied them to the aid station, where he had his own wound dressed. The corpsmen wanted to evacuate him. "Hell no, it isn't

bad," he told them and rejoined his company. Hundreds of yards away, on Shepherd's right, Melvin Krulewitch manned a lonely outpost in front of the 6th Marines. "I said to myself, 'Well, this is what you wanted, isn't it? You wanted the Marine Corps, and now you've got it. You wanted to fight in the war, now you've got it.' You'd look up at the stars at night and you'd think of them looking down at your mother, and you'd get a little homesick. Then your relief would come breaking up your reverie—and you were back in the Marine Corps."

The German advance was an arrow aimed directly at Les Mares Farm. Shepherd said, "It was a key position, as we realized and all we had was a thin red line of Marines with a man about every ten feet apart. A Marine with a rifle—that's all in the hell we had, but we held our lines." The brigade commander sent a stand-and-hold message: "General Harbord directs that the necessary steps be taken to hold our present position at *all costs.*"

German infantry of the 460th Regiment advanced—five hundred, four hundred, three hundred yards—until they closed to within one hundred yards of the hastily dug foxholes, where highly trained riflemen waited for the order to fire. The Marines sighted in, carefully aligning the front sight blade of their .03 rifle on the target's center of mass—a German chest.

Private Elton E. Mackin, 67th Company, 5th Marine Regiment, described his experience of the engagement from a third-person perspective in *Suddenly We Didn't Want to Die*: "Experimentally, he raised his rifle to cover one of those forms. They were so like the silhouette targets of the rifle range at, say, six hundred yards. When glimpsed through the small aperture of a peep sight they were nearly identical in outline, the chest-high figures of men, their heads and shoulders rising above the flood of waving grain through which they came." Hours and hours of practice on the rifle range had made them marksmen, but the targets had been paper; now the silhouettes in front of them were flesh and blood. There was nothing to do but fall back on training: "Target—the half-drawn breath—a finger pressure—recoil. . . . The German staggered and seemed to sag suddenly, wearily, so close that one could see the shock of dumb surprise on [his] face. A hand flung out, instinctive, to ease the fall; then, the figure settled, limp, at rest, pillowed in broken grain."

Wise watched from his PC. "A long way off over those grain fields I could see thin lines of infantry advancing. It wasn't the mass formation I had expected to see after what I had heard of German attacks. Those lines were well extended. At least six or seven paces of open space were between the men. There seemed to be four or five lines, about twenty-five yards apart. They wore the 'coal-shuttle' helmet. Their rifles, bayonets fixed, were at the ready.

"Suddenly, when the German front line was about a hundred yards from us, we opened up. Up and down the line I could see my men working their rifle bolts. I looked for the front line of Germans. There wasn't any!" The deadly accurate rifle fire stopped the attackers in their tracks. "The Boche fell by the scores there among the wheat and the poppies."

The extraordinarily stiff resistance was entirely unexpected by the Germans, who were flushed with victory after having thoroughly trounced the French. They expected it to be a cakewalk to Paris. The first two German waves made repeated attempts to close with the Marines, but every time they came within range, deadly rifle fire forced them back. Dead and wounded carpeted the

This German soldier suffered a fatal head wound. It appears that his helmet was pierced, as was his gas mask container.
Marine Corps History Division

In the intense combat, the dead lay where they had fallen. There was no time to collect the bodies—and often the remains were not discovered until much later. Ten years after Belleau Wood, a French farmer found the skeleton remains of two Marines in the cellar of an abandoned building. *Marine Corps History Division*

ground, attesting to the accuracy of the sharp-shooters. The third wave withdrew, unwilling to cross the field of death. This unexpected setback caused the enemy to stop, consolidate their positions, and bring up reserves. Catlin boasted that "the French, who were in support of the 5th [Marines], could not, and cannot today, grasp the rifle fire of the Marines. That men should fire deliberately and use their sights, and adjust their range, was beyond their experience."

Shepherd expressed concern about a three-hundred-yard gap "between our company and the next battalion in line." As the hard-pressed French withdrew, one of their commanders reported to Shepherd. "They were colonial troops, in khaki uniforms. I assigned them to fill in the gap on our left." Just as the Germans started their attack, he tried to find the French platoon. "I went over to a few trees that were standing on the other side of the farm and looked around, but I couldn't find the French. The Germans opened fire, so I jumped behind a tree, just as the damned missing French platoon started firing. They had withdrawn a couple of hundred yards and now bullets were coming from both directions. There I was, jumping from one side of the tree to the other, trying to keep from getting hit. It was a real

hot spot!" Suddenly, his orderly yelped and jerked convulsively. A French bullet had hit him in the foot, shattering the bones and making it impossible for him to walk. Shepherd half-carried the wounded private to a frontline aid station before returning to the company.

Upon returning, Shepherd learned that several gray-coated figures had been spotted creeping through the waist-high wheat. He placed snipers on top of a haystack to pick off the German infiltrators. "The wheat in the field to their front was waist high but we could see the Germans moving in the wheat." Shepherd sent out a half-dozen men under Gunnery Sgt. David L. Buford, who "had seen plenty of bushwhacking in Haiti. Our patrol surprised the German patrol and killed about a dozen of them. Sergeant Buford, who was a wonderful pistol shot, killed seven Germans alone with his automatic." Shepherd recalled Buford returning "with a grin on his face. 'Lieutenant,' he chuckled, 'I think I got seven.' So, I went over to see, and there they were, laid out like cordwood. That stopped the infiltration in this area." During the night, a detachment of machine gunners drove off the enemy infantry.

All night long and into the morning, German artillery fire blanketed the farms and wood lines,

The introduction of the machine gun changed the entire dimension of warfare. Unfortunately, the tactics of the day—massed infantry attacks—were slow in recognizing its significance. Thousands of men were thrown against defenses that were in essence impervious to assault. *Marine Corps History Division*

suspecting the Americans were using them for shelter and PCs. Sergeant Don Paradis, 80th Company, was just "about to have breakfast from my reserve ration when a shell came through the roof of the barn wounding several men. The rest rushed out of the big double doors onto the crushed rock road, toward the woods. A shell lit right in the middle of them, killing seven and wounding ten or twelve. They lay on both sides of the road. Top Sergeant Frank L. Glick was lying on his stomach, both legs cut off just above the knees. My friend Fred Lomax shouted for help. His leg was broken near the hip and lay at right angles to his side. He kept trying to rise up. I could see from the gray look on his face that he was in shock. I threw my pack and rifle on the ground and yelled, 'My God, who will help me with these men?'"

The Americans dug emplacements "deep enough to stand up in," consolidating and strengthening their positions until they were "damn near impregnable." They brought up artillery—"the 75mm guns were lined up wheel to wheel"—to provide counterbattery fire and to work over the enemy frontline positions. Machine guns were fully integrated into the defense, "being moved around to where more firepower was needed." Victor Bleasdale's section of Hotchkiss machine guns "covered a gap in the line, a clear field, of about several hundred acres and between six and eight hundred yards wide." A French straggler happened by. "*Où est le Boche?* [Where is the Boche?]," Bleasdale asked. The Frenchman replied, "*Regardez vous!*" and gestured. "I looked over to where he pointed and saw the Germans advancing down a slope through a wheat field. 'Jesus Christ,' I exclaimed, and opened fire on them."

The enemy pounded the Americans with artillery, while probing their positions with small parties of infantry to find weak points. The Germans sent back dismal reports. "Five rifle companies in the 47th Regiment were fighting without officers; on June 4, the 398th Regiment reported an average company strength of 40 men and these 'were not fit for frontline service'; the 6th Grenadier Regiment reported itself 'exhausted and incapable of further effort'; the division artillery 'was worn out'; the division commander estimated a total loss of 2,700 to 3,000 men."

Finally, on June 5, the German commander, von Contra, had had enough and called off the attack. He ordered his exhausted men to dig in. "Group Contra is compelled temporarily to assume the defensive. Severe measures will be taken against individuals who . . . go to the rear."

Hundreds of dramatic recruiting and home-front posters produced to inspire patriotism decorated homes and public buildings throughout the country. This poster, "Over the Top," used a term first coined by the British to signify attacking out of their trenches. *Marine Corps History Division*

Chapter 5

Over the Top to Hill 142

Marine Brigade Field Order No. 1 issued at 10:25 p.m., June 5: 1st Battalion, 5th Marines, supported by 8th and 23rd Machine Gun companies, will attack at 3:45 a.m. to seize Hill 142. Hill 142, a tree-covered ridge running two kilometers generally north to south, was flanked by dry streambeds, heavy with thick undergrowth. The ridge itself was a jumble of dense underbrush and boulder-strewn, undulating terrain that provided a perfect defense. The northern portion of the ridge and the eastern edge were steep and

Ground over which the 1st Battalion, 5th Marines, advanced to capture Hill 142. There was not a shred of cover to protect the advancing Marines from the deadly German machine guns. *Marine Corps History Division*

Private Elton E. Mackin joined the 1st Battalion, 5th Marines, in time for their attack on Hill 142. He became a company runner, one of the "suicide squad," and managed to survive some of the most vicious fighting of the war. For heroic achievement, he was awarded the Army Distinguished Service Cross, the Navy Cross, and two Silver Star citations. *Elton E. Mackin,* Suddenly We Didn't Want to Die

covered with bush. A three-hundred-meter waist-high wheat field sloped gently upward from the Marine position to the crest of the pine-covered hill.

By three o'clock on the morning of June 6, the brigade was organized: the 1st and 2nd battalions of the 5th Regiment and the 2nd and 3rd battalions of the 6th Regiment formed the frontline. The 2nd Battalion of the 5th Regiment and the 1st Battalion of the 6th Regiment made up the reserves. The companies of the 6th Machine Gun Battalion were distributed among the battalions on the front.

The German defense of Hill 142 placed three fresh companies of the 237th Infantry Division squarely in the path of the Marine attack. Additional reserves were located within easy striking distance to be used as a counterattack force. Each company had an effective strength of between ninety and one hundred men and had six light and two heavy machine guns within its table of organization. The men holding Hill 142 were not considered attack troops. Rather, they were specially trained "sector-holding" troops, whose sole job was to defend and hold critical terrain.

Captain John Thomason's poetic description of the enemy is well worth quoting. "A company of German infantry and a machine gun platoon lay in the three-cornered clump of trees on the forward slopes of Hill 142. . . . By the white piping on their uniforms, they were Prussians, and by the ugly, confident look of them, with a touch of Berlin swank, they were Prussians of a vcry good division; and there were no better soldiers in the world."

Just before dawn the word was passed from foxhole to foxhole, "Standby to move out." The chilled, sleepy men got to their feet, shouldered their weapons, and cautiously moved to the edge of the woods, 49th Company (Capt. George W. Hamilton) on the right, 67th Company (1st Lt. Orlando C. Crowther) on the left. "We were all lined up behind our lines," one private wrote. "In front of us lay a large open field and in front of that a thickly wooded hill. That was where we were going. We all had kind of a funny feeling, but we laid back there smoking and telling jokes while we waited for the order to form. Well, at daybreak we commenced to form."

Private Mackin was "rudely interrupted by authority in the person of Gunnery Sergeant Eilers, who said flatly, 'Fix your bayonets!' The order was a complete surprise, startling and appalling in its potentiality."

The battalion commander, Maj. Julius S. "Old Jule" Turrill, a tough old Corps regular, ordered them to advance even though two of his companies failed to show up. (The 66th and 17th companies were still in line at Les Mares Farm waiting for the French to relieve them.) Pvt. Macklin described how "First Sergeant 'Pop' Hunter, the 67th Company's top-cutter, strode out into the field and, a soldier to the last, threw a competent glance right and left, noting the dress of his company line. Pop was an old man, not only of portly figure and graying hair but in actual years—far more than thirty years of service lay behind him. His cane swung overhead and forward, pointing toward the first objective, a thousand yards of wheat away: the tensely quiet edge of German-

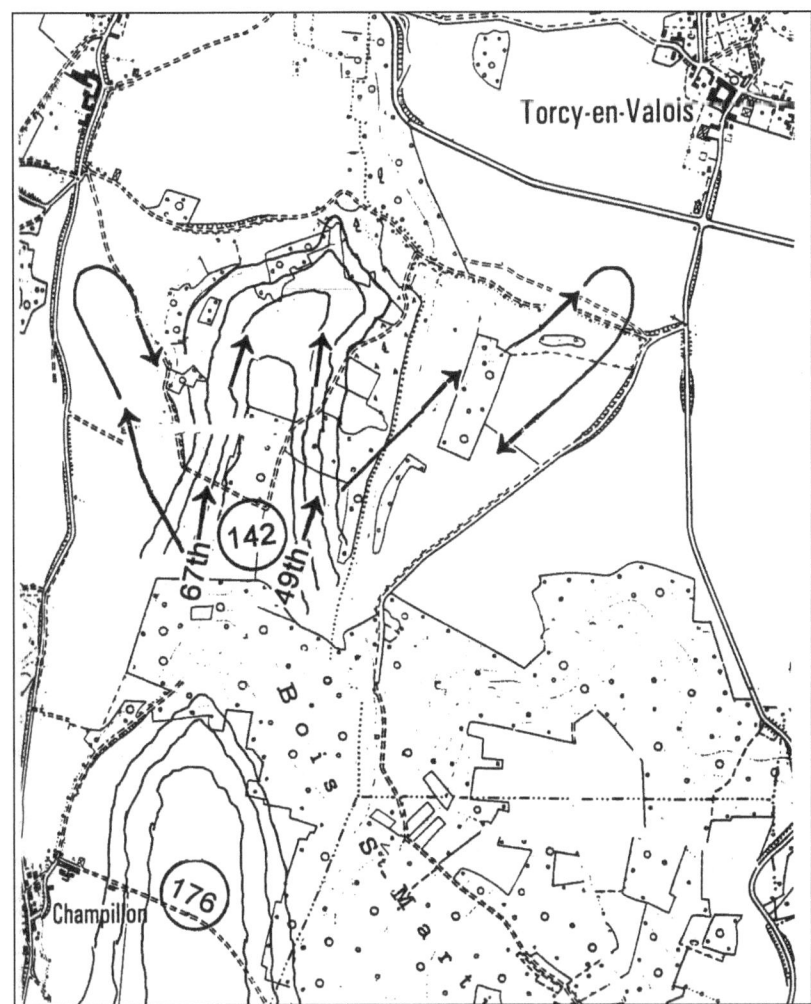

Two companies of the 1st Battalion, 5th Marines, were ordered to attack Hill 142 early on the morning of June 6, 1918, in the Marine Brigade's first offensive action of the war. Five hundred Marines went "over the top" to seize the hill. *Northwest of Chateau Thierry: 1 June–10 July (unpublished 2nd Division report)*

held Belleau Wood. . . . A single burst of shrapnel came to meet the moving line of men. There was a scream of pain, a plaintive cry of hurt. In some alarm, a soldier yelled, 'Hey Pop, there's a man hit over here.' Pop's reply was terse and pungent: 'C'mon, goddamnit! He ain't the last man who's gonna be hit today.' "

The two companies advanced at foot-pace through an open field of waist-high wheat and meadows, little copses and shallow ravines—"guiding center with great care"—toward the tree-covered ridge. Floyd Gibbons wrote, "There are really no heroics about it. There is no bugle call, no sword waving, no theatricalism—it's just plain

Observation Balloons

Balloons were used by aerial observers to plot the enemy's position and for calling in artillery fire. For this last reason, the "gas bags," as they were known, were universally hated by the infantrymen of all nations. From their "lofty" position—between one thousand and four thousand feet, the observers used binoculars to locate targets, and then communicated the information to the firing batteries by wireless. Every effort was made to shoot down the high-value targets, but each side went to great lengths to protect them. The balloon was highly defended, always surrounded by skillful machine gunners and antiaircraft cannon. Often pursuit planes waited in ambush, pouncing out of the sun. The secret to being a successful "balloon buster" was to sneak up on them, fire quickly, and get the heck out of the area—if you were lucky.

Marines train to use an observation balloon. Many of the balloons were cylindrical, earning them the nickname "sausages." *Marine Corps History Division*

The gas bags were filled with highly flammable hydrogen, which quickly became a torch when hit with tracers. For this reason the observers were issued parachutes. However, the parachutes had a high failure rate, so they were used only in dire emergencies. If an attacker was spotted in time, the ground crew quickly reeled the observer in—often within a minute. Nevertheless, 241 German observation balloons were shot down during the war.

Short, stocky, and dark complexioned, Maj. Julius S. Turrill was appointed a second lieutenant in 1899 and subsequently served in the Philippines, Cuba, Guam, and aboard ship. For extraordinary heroism during World War I, he was awarded the Distinguished Service Cross, the Navy Cross, the French Legion of Honor, the French Croix de Guerre with two Bronze Stars and two Palms, and four American Expeditionary Citations. He retired in 1932 as a colonel and advanced to the rank of brigadier general in 1942 on the retired list. *Marine Corps History Division*

get up and go over. And it is done just the same as one would walk across a peaceful wheat field out in Iowa." Four waves of Marines, "walking ankle deep in ground mist, rifles loaded, bayonets fixed, their eyes on the exploding terrain through which they soon must pass."

Lieutenant John W. Thomason Jr. watched the line of Marines come out of the tree line. "The light was strong when they advanced into the open wheat, now all starred with dewy poppies, red as blood."

As the assault waves left the cover of the woods, they were spotted by German balloon observers, who could then relay the location to German artillery. General Harbord complained to the division commander. "There is hardly a turn in the line or a portion of the road from which one or more German balloons in not plainly visible. I can see four German balloons from my headquarters. Any activity or appearance of people along that line in sight of these balloons is followed within a very few minutes by shell fire."

John Thomason wrote his father, "By far the most Christianizing influence that I have run across . . . is the German 77mm shell shrapnel or HE (high explosive), which is the stuff that strafes you in your position—when your line is posted and all you can do is to lie low and make yourself as small as possible. You can hear the cursed things coming, a tearing whine that rises to a shrieking crescendo—then the burst. O, Lord, that was close! O, Lord, don't let it hit me!"

Merwin Silverthorn remembered holding a bayoneted rifle as he moved "at a slow steady cadence that we had been taught . . . in trench warfare formation with rifles at 'high port,' not even firing. On our left, approximately two hundred yards, was a little rocky place—an eminence—teaming with machine guns and nobody, literally nobody, was firing a shot at those Germans. They had us enfiladed. It was like a shooting gallery and not a single Marine of ours was firing a shot."

Thomason described how "the platoons, assailed now by a fury of small-arms fire, narrowed their eyes and inclined their bodies forward, like men in a heavy rain, and went on." Casualties were heavy; Pop Hunter was "one of the first. Hit twice and up twice, hit the third time, he went down for good."

Captain Hamilton "had not moved fifty yards when they cut loose at us from the woods ahead—more machine guns than I had ever heard before. Our men had been trained on a special method of [avoiding] machine guns, and, according to their training, all immediately lay down flat—some fell." First Lieutenant S. C. Cumming hated the Germans because "The Hun machine gunners fire low, as after you are hit in the leg you fall and then they fill your body with bullets, so there is little chance." Cumming was hit and "spun around and hit flat. I crawled to a shell-hole. . . . I don't know how I got there, as the ground was being plowed by machine guns. I heard later that my company had one officer and twenty-nine men left. We had gone in with eight officers and two hundred and fifty men."

Burial Detail

A burial detail, led by a chaplain, carries a body to the cemetery after the battle. It was gruesome business; decomposition and dismemberment added to the burden. *Marine Corps History Division*

An old-timer passing by on business of his own stopped to watch. Occasionally . . . the observer's hand flicked upward in salute. After a time, as the work progressed, a body was handed down dressed in forest greens with a top-cutter's chevrons above hashmarks, denoting seven enlistments. A whistle dangled loosely from a cord about the sergeant's neck, and the flap of his holster flopped about untidily. The old-timer, still watching, made a sharp salute. Turning to a boot [a young Marine] he said, "Get a blanket soldier. Wrap him up proper. That's 'Pop' Hunter."
—Pvt. Elton E. Mackin

Hamilton had "vague recollections of urging [my] men on—of grouping prisoners and sending them to the rear under one man instead of several—of snatching an iron cross ribbon off the first officer I got—and of shooting wildly at several retreating Boches. Farther on, we came to an open field—a wheat field full of red poppies—and here we caught hell. We rushed across the open and found out why it was so hot for us. Three machine-gun companies were holding down these woods and the infantry were farther back." Lieutenant Crowther of the 49th took a machine-gun bullet in the arm but kept going with his men, refusing to give up command.

Prisoners offer a valuable source of intelligence, and both sides attempted to capture enemy soldiers alive. However, in the heat of combat, at close quarters in hand-to-hand combat, it was often not possible to take prisoners.
Morgan Dennis, Dear Folks at Home

Merwin Silverthorn and his platoon commander made it to a ravine and took cover. The officer looked around and said, "Where the hell is my platoon?" Silverthorn shouted, "There's only six of us left. All the rest have been killed, wounded, or pinned down." The lieutenant told Silverthorn that he was going back and told him to stick with him. "Here's where you and I part company," Silverthorn thought, "because we just got across that place and that's the last thing I'm going to do is go back. Nobody ever got in trouble for going toward the enemy."

The two split up; Silverthorn joined up with the remnants of another platoon commanded by a gunnery sergeant. "The sergeant got wounded, shot through the shoulder blade, and I bound his wound. So now I was in command of a few people. We started advancing by rushes, as fast and as far as we could, until we dropped from exhaustion. About

the second rush, when I dropped to the ground, it felt like I'd hit my knee on a rock. It felt as if somebody had hit me with a baseball bat right across the kneecap—a terrific blow, but fortunately no pain. A machine-gun bullet had creased my knee. It was stiff and I couldn't run." By this time there were only two of them. Silverthorn told the other Marine to go ahead; he was needed in the woods. Silverthorn decided to "stay right where I am until it's dark and I can get out under cover of darkness."

Lieutenant Victor Bleasdale watched as a "couple of Marines came along with a German officer prisoner. He was the most overbearing son-of-a-bitch I had ever seen. He wore a smart-looking uniform, spic and span—I don't know how the hell he kept it so clean. He looked over at me like I was a worm and yelled haughtily in English, 'Chin up.' I felt like shooting the son-of-a-bitch!"

"We got a lot of prisoners and they were mighty glad to be captured, at least they said they were," Cpl. H. A. Leonard indignantly recalled. "I was talking to one who said that he was going to come to the United States after the war. I told him to get that idea entirely out of his head, as we were going to lynch them as fast as they come. Just two hours before he had been mowing our men down, and now he figured on going to America. Can you beat that?"

Despite the intense machine-gun fire and heavy casualties, the inflamed Marines overran the German machine-gun positions and, with hideous yells, they bayoneted the gunners and their supporting infantry. "They must have thought from the way we were shooting and yelling that the whole American army was coming through the woods," a bayonet-toting victor laughed, "and came out with their hands up, yelling, *'Kamerad, Kamerad.'* "

A company commander reported that he "could hear our men in the woods bellowing, 'Get that son-of-a-bitch' and similar remarks." One Marine wrote home, "A Hun struck at me with his bayonet. I could not defend myself with my gun at the moment as a branch was in the way. I parried the thrust with my left arm, let go of my gun, ducked, and uppercut the fellow hard. He fell back stunned. With the knife I had in my leggings, I finished him neatly, recovered my gun, and went on."

Gunnery Sergeant Charles F. Hoffman, a quiet forty-year-old career Marine, saw a line of Germans

The Marines who survived the terrible slaughter in the wheat field took the bayonet to the German machine gunners. The wood became an abattoir—in many cases the two enemies locked in a fatal embrace. *Morgan Dennis,* Dear Folks at Home

crawling through the heavy brush, dragging five light machine guns. He realized that if they got into firing position they would sweep the Marines off the hill. With a bloodcurdling yell, he launched a bayonet assault. "A short thrust killed the lead German. Pulling back the dripping blade, the lithe sergeant whirled and caught the next man." Other Marines joined the fray and dispersed the remaining Germans.

The remnants of the assault companies pressed forward. Hamilton explained, "In the excitement and eagerness in chasing the Boche the men went very fast." Thomason recalled, "They went down the brushy slope, across a little run, across a road where two heavy Maxim [machine guns] were caught sitting, and mopped up and up the next long smooth slope."

"Afterwards we found out why it was they made it so hot for us—three [German] machine-

Gunnery Sgt. Ernest August Janson

Gunnery Sgt. Ernest A. Janson, one of only five Marines to receive both the Army and Navy Medals of Honor during World War I. *Marine Corps History Division*

Gunnery Sergeant Ernest A. Janson, aka Charles F. Hoffman, enlisted under an alias to avoid the stigma of a German-sounding name. He received the Croix de Guerre with palm, the French Military Cross, and the Purple Heart.

Janson was awarded both the Army and Navy Medals of Honor for the same incident on Hill 142. The Army Medal of Honor citation reads: "For conspicuous gallantry and intrepidity above and beyond the call of duty in action with the enemy near Chateau-Thierry, France, June 6, 1918. Immediately after the company to which he belonged had reached its objective in Hill 142, several hostile counterattacks were launched against the line before the new position had been consolidated. Sergeant Janson was attempting to organize a position on the north slope of the hill when he saw twelve of the enemy, armed with five light machine guns, crawling toward his group. Giving the alarm, he rushed the hostile detachment, bayoneted the two leaders, and forced the others to flee, abandoning their guns. His quick action, initiative, and courage drove the enemy from a position from which they could have swept the hill with machine-gun fire and forced the withdrawal of our troops."

The Marines took cover in the old German trenches or quickly scrapped one of their own. Getting below the ground meant the difference between life and death. The crack of bullets and grenade explosions became a roar, blocking out the senses. *Marine Corps History Division*

gun companies were holding down these woods and the infantry were farther back," George Hamilton explained wondrously. "Besides several of the heavy Maxims we later found several empty belts and a dead gunner sitting on the seat or lying nearby. It was only because we rushed the positions that we were able to take them."

Crowther of the 67th was hit a second time in the throat by a sniper and fell mortally wounded. Hamilton, one of the few surviving officers "started getting the two companies together." The situation was desperate. He sent a frantic message to Turrill. "Elements of this company and 67th are on the nose of Hill 142 . . . very much disorganized . . . our position not very good. We are entrenching . . . have been counterattacked several times . . . casualties very heavy, we badly need medical aid and many hospital apprentices. Ammunition of all kinds needed . . . will need artillery to hold this line . . . all my officers are gone."

Hamilton's surviving riflemen dug in and fought for their lives. German infantry filtered through the trees. Thomason eloquently recorded the heroic defense. "The Boche wanted Hill 142;

No-man's-land, as viewed from the lines established by 1st Battalion, 5th Marines, after the capture of Hill 142. *Marine Corps History Division*

he came, and the rifles broke him, and he came again. All his batteries were in action, and always his machine guns scourged the place, but he could not make headway against the rifles . . . aimed, sustained rifle fire . . . demoralized him."

A letter taken from an enemy body was translated. "The Americans are savages. They kill

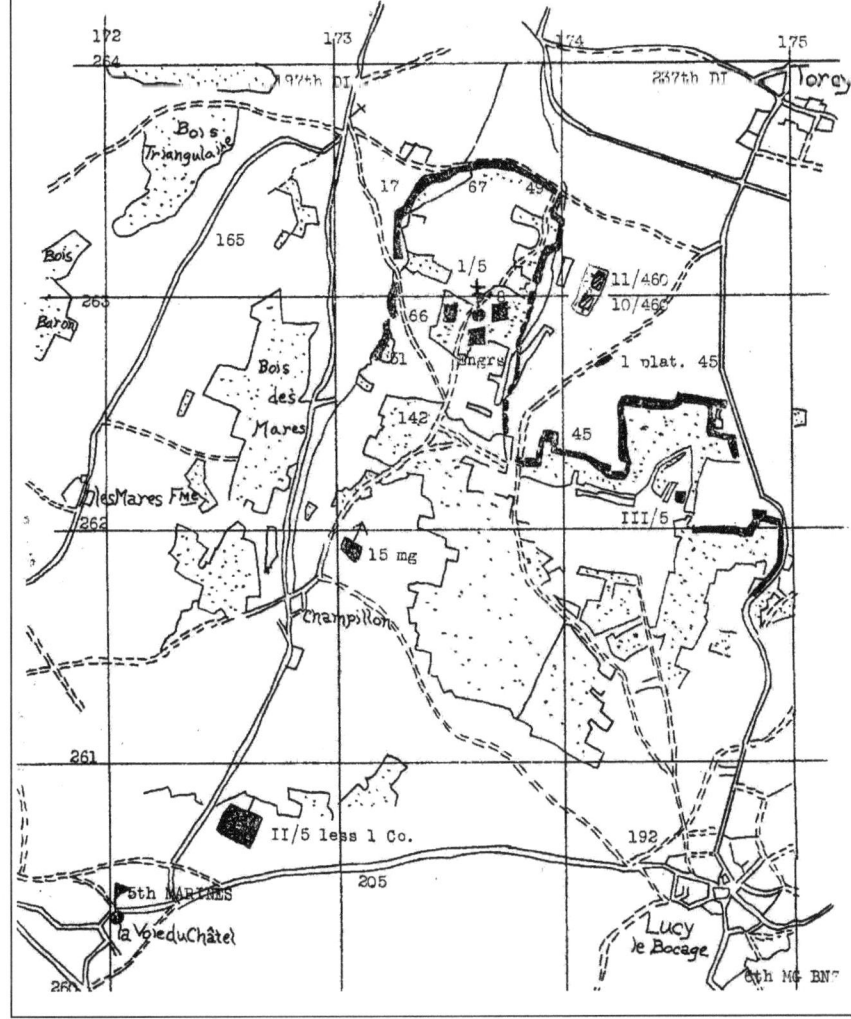

Turrill's advance beyond Hill 142 had been accomplished at great cost and created a bubble in the line that the Germans were attempting to capitalize on. His men were under considerable pressure from direct attack as well as by mortar and artillery fire. *Northwest of Chateau Thierry: 1 June–10 July (unpublished 2nd Division report)*

off the hill—but—we held on," Hamilton proudly announced. "One especially came near getting me. There were heavy bushes all over the hill, and the first thing I knew hand grenades began dropping nearby. One grenade threw a rock which caught me behind the ear and made me dizzy for a few minutes." The combined firepower of the four companies was enough to stop the Germans. An emotionally charged Hamilton bragged, "The Boche haven't a chance as long as they are up against Marines!"

Captain John Thomason proudly stated, "I am one of the very few men alive who threw the 28th Prussian—Brandenburgers—off that hill and kept them off."

By midday Turrill's lines were stabilized but not strongly held. He sent a field message to Neville at 11:45. "We have reached our objective and are entrenching. The line of trenches facing east from the junction of the ravines on our right—Williams is up on the left with three platoons, Hamilton in center, and Winans on right—the remnants of other companies have joined the other two. . . . Shelling is severe at present." His battalion had suffered a heavy cost to take the hill, 8 officers and 325 men. Hamilton's company lost 90 percent of its officers and 50 percent of its enlisted men, killed or wounded. Turrill's advance created a salient more than a kilometer long and less than a kilometer wide, and he was worried. "A strong attack on our right will finish us."

everything that moves." A Marine proudly wrote home that the Germans "call us 'devil dogs,' '*Teufelhunden,*' in German."

Reinforcements rushed forward "through woods that were just covered with dead Marines and Germans." Turrill shoved Capt. Raymond P. Dirkson's 66th Company into the center of the line across the top of the hill; he had Lloyd Williams' 51st Company tie in with the 67th and deployed Capt. Roswell Winan's 17th Company on the right of the shattered 49th Company, forming a line west of the hill, facing at right angles to the advance. Lieutenant Robert Blake "found a ravine, extending north and south, toward the front, filled with German dead. I brought up the 17th Company without any losses. After that, I could do no wrong!"

The Germans launched several counterattacks. "Five nasty ones that came near driving us back

With the Second Division

The Americans stood tall, eager to prove themselves to the Boche and avenge the atrocities the Germans were alleged to have committed. *Charles Baldridge–National Museum of the Marine Corps*

CHAPTER 6

Nothing but Marines in the Town of Bouresches

As the struggle for Hill 142 continued, Major Holcomb's 2nd Battalion, 6th Marines, on the right, spent time cleaning rifles, redistributing ammunition, and preparing for action. Sergeant Don Paradis "was kept busy with running messages to various company commanders. We knew action was planned." Suddenly, a motorcycle roared up. The dust-covered messenger handed Colonel Catlin the succinct attack order. "Seize the village of Bouresches and the railroad station."

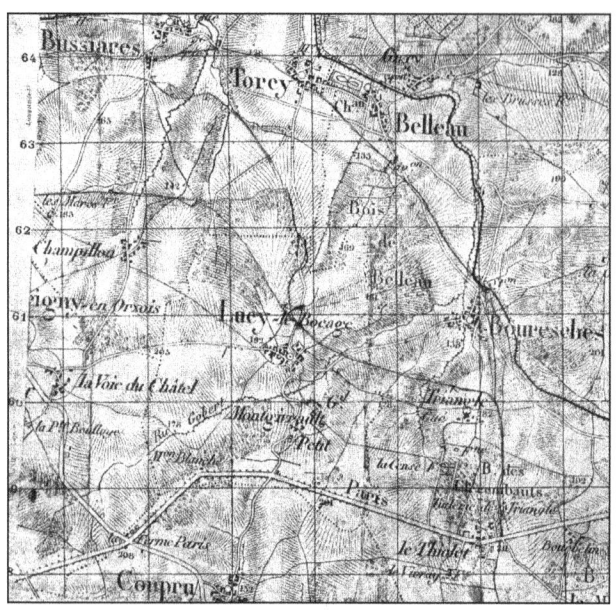

Maps were in scarce supply, and lucky was the company commander who had one. Often they were large-scale maps and did not offer much in the way of detail, which led to confusion as to location both at the unit level and higher headquarters. *Northwest of Chateau Thierry: 1 June–10 July (unpublished 2nd Division report)*

Below: The small village of Bouresches consisted of thirty to forty two-story brick houses located on an east/west road between Lucy-le-Bocage and Vaux, three-quarters of a mile from the southern lobe of Belleau Wood. Another dirt road ran from the village north to Belleau. Most of its thousand-some inhabitants took to their heels upon news of the German approach. They had left everything except what little valuables they could carry on their backs or in small carts, forming a pitiful procession fleeing the Boche.

After they left, Bouresches was heavily shelled. "Dead cows, Boche, cats, and most anything lying around. The streets are full of debris, and what's left of the houses is a grand mess of household goods strewn everywhere, mingled with china, vegetables, and what-not." A battalion of the German 10th Division defended the village, using the empty shells of buildings as cover for machine gunners and snipers. *Patrick Mooney*

Lieutenant John A. West doubled-timed to the company headquarters, where he found his commander, Capt. Randolph Zane and several other officers grouped around a map lying on the ground. Zane outlined the attack, which was to kick off at 5:00 p.m. "We were to follow Major Sibley's 3rd Battalion, keeping a distance of five hundred yards between us. Murray's platoon was to attack from the other side, following Captain Duncan's 96th Company." Second Lieutenant Clifton B. "Cliff" Cates, one of Duncan's platoon commanders, wrote, "At 4:35 p.m., we received word that we were to move in to position and to attack a certain town [Bouresches] at 5 p.m. The entire line was to move forward—the town was my company's objective." Sergeant Glen G. Hill could see "a huge Zeppelin over Belleau Wood that was directing German artillery fire."

Cliff Cates was called to the PC. "About 4:45 p.m., Capt. Donald F. Duncan received orders that the 96th Company was to attack. He called the officers together and gave us what information he had, and then the company assembled and marched down the ravine west of Triangle Farm. Three platoons took up positions in the woods six hundred meters southwest of Bouresches. The fourth platoon was just to the west behind a knoll in a wheat field."

Battalion runner Paradis watched "as zero hour approached and our companies moved out in wave formation. Headquarters formed as well, with Major Holcomb and Adjutant Perry Wilmer in the center. Colonel Albertus W. Catlin shook hands with Major Holcomb, and then the word

was given to move forward." Minutes later Catlin was shot. "It felt exactly as though some one had struck me heavily with a sledge. It swung me clear around and toppled me over on the ground. When I tried to get up I found that my right side was paralyzed." Captain Laspiere, the French liaison officer, reported the incident to Harbord. "Catlin wounded five hours thirty-seven minutes. Have sent runner to Feland (second in command of 5th Marines) to take command." Harbord ignored Laspiere and designated Lt. Col. Harry Lee to take Catlin's place.

The men advanced down a slope to a field covered with waist-high wheat. Paradis noted that "all was quiet until the advancing boys were within range. The enemy opened up with their machine guns and one-pounder cannons and artillery fire. They had held it until they could put a barrage down just in front of their lines." West and his platoon were in the wheat field, advancing by "squad rushes, flopping down at intervals. Machine-gun fire from Belleau Woods was taking its toll. We were now among wounded and dead of Major Sibley's battalion. The wounded were crying for aid and stretcher bearers. There were none. I remember trying to stop a wounded man's bleeding. He had been shot through both legs. He was just a kid, crying hard. I had to go but I came back to find during my absence that a shell had blown off both his legs and he was dead."

Cliff Cates and his men "deployed across this wheat field, taking very heavy fire." Erskine's platoon was pinned down and couldn't advance. He told a wounded man to inform Captain Zane of

Vigorous Col. W. Albertus Catlin, commanding 6th Marines, moved forward to watch the attack on Belleau Wood, despite the warning of his staff. He took a position on a small rise about three hundred yards from the woods, screened by a clump of bushes. As he watched the attack through field glasses, a German sniper shot him in the chest, puncturing his right lung. His French liaison officer pulled him to cover. *Marine Corps History Division*

The church in the center of town was merely a shell, its interior gutted by high-explosive shell fire. German artillery targeted the town in an effort to loosen the grip of its Marine defenders. In addition, errant American long-range cannon pumped shells into it despite the pleas to stop. *Patrick Mooney*

his predicament. The man returned. "I told the captain what you said and he told me to tell you to 'Get going, goddamnit!' Zane was a pretty tough character," and Erskine "got going."

Meanwhile, Cates learned that his company commander was dead. Sergeant Hill was about twenty yards from the officer when he was killed. "Captain Duncan walked out of the woods, tapping his leg with his swagger stick. Suddenly there was an explosion and a heavy burst of machine-gun fire. Captain Duncan sank to the ground. Two corpsmen and Lieutenant Osborne ran over to help. As they bent over, a shell burst killed them all." Lieutenant James F. Robinson the executive officer took command. Cates "saw him jump up in front of the woods, wave his pistol, and shout 'Come on.' The 2nd, 3rd, and 4th platoons formed a skirmish line and started toward Bouresches, keeping up a running fire. The 2nd Platoon laid down about two hundred yards from the village and fired away, trying to gain fire superiority. However, the German fire was so hot that the 2nd and 3rd platoons took refuge in the ravine to the right."

As Cates ran across the field, a machine-gun bullet struck his helmet and he collapsed to the ground unconscious. "I soon regained consciousness," he recalled, "and saw Lieutenant Robertson

with my platoon entering the western part of the town and begin a savage house-to-house fight. . . . [I tried to put my helmet on,] but it wouldn't fit because there was a big dent in it as big as your fist. I staggered to my feet—I fell two or three times—and got in a ravine with three other Marines." Private Tom Argaut saw Cates' condition and started to pour wine from his canteen over his head. "Goddamn it, Tom," Cates told him, "don't pour that wine over my head, give me a drink of it."

Cates staggered forward, groggy from the blow to the head. "I saw a few men just in front who were firing on the town with a Chauchat, and the Germans were running out. I took the men into the town and set up a machine-gun position. All the Germans had gotten out with the exception of a few who occupied the northern edge. About that time I saw Robertson. I yelled and blew my whistle to get his attention. He came over and said, 'All right, you take the platoon in and clean out the town, and I'll go get reinforcements,' which I thought was a hell of a thing—because the damn town still had a hell of a lot of Germans. We took heavy fire going down the streets, in fact, a bullet punched a hole through my helmet and another hit me in the shoulder." As Cates and his small band advanced, they ran into a German machine-

Second Lieutenant Clifton B. "Cliff" Cates was instrumental in taking Bouresches. Knocked out when a machine-gun bullet struck his helmet, he led his men into the town after he came to. *Marine Corps History Division*

Above and Beyond

Distinguished Service Cross citation, Capt. Randolph T. Zane: "While in command of American forces in a captured town . . . he was attacked by heavy machine-gun fire and by infantry. His successful handling of the defense and his personal example of bravery and coolness inspired the garrison to resist with such effect that, although the infantry were at one time within 30 feet of the town, the town was held and the enemy repulsed with heavy losses."

Medal of Honor citation, Dental Surgeon Weedon C. Osborne U.S.N.: "Risked his life to aid the wounded when the advance upon the enemy of June 6th was temporarily checked by a hail of machine-gun fire. He helped carry Captain Donald F. Duncan to a place of safety, when that officer was wounded, and had almost reached it when a shell killed them both. Having joined the regiment but a few days before its entry into the line, and being new to the service, he displayed heroism worthy of its best traditions."

The debris from destroyed houses provided cover for the German defenders. The Marines had to dig them out, at a heavy cost. The fighting was close—hand grenade range—which left little option for taking prisoners. *Patrick Mooney*

German machine gunners moving into position. The Germans rushed reinforcements into the village, but they were too late; the Marines had established a foothold that could not be loosened. *Marine Corps History Division*

Marine reinforcements used the defilade provided by the creek to get into the village. The stream in June was a mere trickle, unlike this photo. *Marine Corps History Division*

gun nest in the church tower, which they silenced with rifle fire. Another gun, on the edge of town, drove them back to cover after wounding six men. "I decided to let it stay there as I only had a very few men left."

Paradis was standing with Major Holcomb when Lieutenant Robertson reported having taken the village. "The major had to direct him to return to help his own men and hold the town. [Major Holcomb] thanked him for coming back . . . but told him that his place was back with his men. We learned later that it was really Lieutenant Cates who had taken the town and organized its defense that night."

Catlin wrote that "Three to four hundred Germans held the town . . . the place bristled with machine guns. There were guns at the street corners, behind barricades, and even on the housetops, but the Marines kept on. They attacked with rifle, bayonet, and grenade. They were outnumbered when they started, and one by one they were put out of the fighting. But they kept going, taking gun after gun, until the Germans, for all their numbers and advantage of position, began to fall back." Cates stated it quite simply, "We cleaned out most of the town but by that time I only had twenty-one men left." Within an hour, though, Captain Zane came in with the remnants of the 79th Company. He sent a lieutenant to the regimental headquarters with a situation report. "Bouresches held by about 100 men of the 96th Company, all of the 79th Company, amounting to about 90 men and 175 men of the 2nd Engineers. The Boche still hold the railroad station."

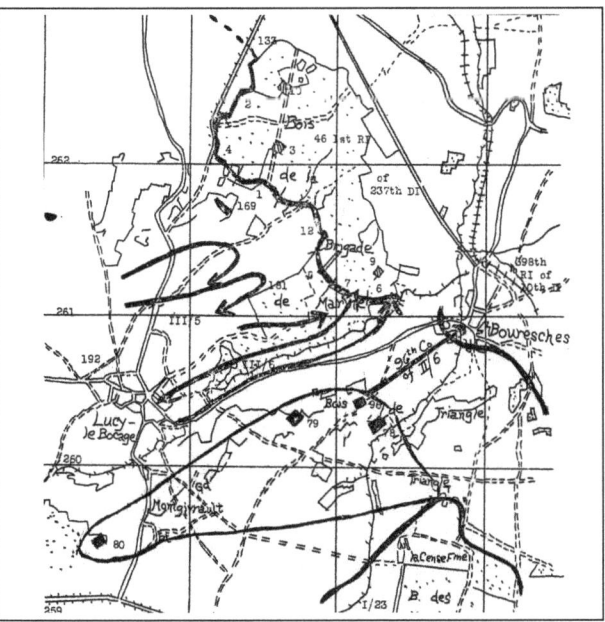

During the Spanish-American War, then Sergeant Quick "distinguished himself by signaling the USS *Dolphin* on three different occasions while exposed to a heavy fire from the enemy." Marine historian Robert D. Heinl wrote, "Quick stood calmly amid U.S. and Spanish fire to wig-wag the *Dolphin* to concentrate on the Spanish positions rather than on ground already captured by the Marines. The novelist Stephen Crane recorded the moment: 'I watched his face, and it was as grave and serene as a man writing his own library. . . . I saw Quick betray only one sign of emotion. As he swung his clumsy flag to and fro, an end of it once caught on a cactus pillar. He looked annoyed.' "

The attack of 96th Company on Bouresches. The company had to cross the hated wheat fields, where many were cut down, but enough made it into the village to wrest it from the Germans. The map also shows the ill-fated attack of 3rd Battalion, 5th Marines, who were forced to turn back, and the more successful 3rd Battalion, 6th Marines, who pushed into Belleau Wood. *Northwest of Chateau Thierry: 1 June–10 July (unpublished 2nd Division report)*

The ammunition situation was desperate. Robertson sent a runner to Holcomb's PC with an urgent request for resupply. Lieutenant William Moore and the old campaigner Sgt. Maj. John Quick volunteered to drive a truckload of ammunition to the beleaguered men. They managed to survive a wild ride along a rutted, shell-pocked road and deliver the vital ammunition. Their truck was peppered with bullets and shrapnel. Both men received the Distinguished Service Cross.

After a harrowing journey, Erskine managed to make it into Bouresches:

When I arrived, Captain Zane was already there. "How many men do you have?" he asked.

"I have five, I think."

[A]s cool as a cucumber he said, "I want you to go out and locate the Germans."

I thought he was kidding and said, "I know where they are, they're all over the goddamn world!"

Without batting an eye he said, "I'm serious, take what you have left of your platoon and go locate the Germans."

So I took off thinking, "By God, this is my last trip, I'm not going to make it."

The patrol succeeded—"when we heard a noise, we threw a rock. If anybody fired back, we figured it was a German"—and got back to Bouresches about three o'clock in the morning.

Cates remembered, "With Zane and his company in the town, there wasn't any question about holding the place. I mean, in two or three hours we had enough men in there to hold half a dozen towns." However, a French pilot from Esquadrille Squadron 252 reported seeing men leaving the village. The French demanded assurances that the Marines were not pulling back. Holcomb, in no mood for their accusations, angrily responded, "When I do any running, it will be in the opposite direction!" Harbord asked the French to investigate the false report, "which is most annoying."

On June 13, Harbord would report, "There is nothing but U.S. Marines in the town of Bouresches." The attack on Bouresches cost hundreds of Marine casualties but, according to Cates, its capture was worth it. "I've often contended, and I'm frankly convinced, if we hadn't gotten Bouresches, we would not have had any chance in Belleau Woods."

Dozens were cut down as the Marines advanced across the open ground. German machine-gun fire was unmerciful—men were hit and hit again as they fell. *John W. Thomason, Jr.,* Fix Bayonets!

Chapter 7

Machine Guns in the Wheat

The Bois de Belleau, Belleau Wood, was an old hunting preserve, covering about a square mile beginning half a kilometer south of Belleau village, and generally elevated above the surrounding wheat fields. The wood, almost two kilometers long from north to south, a kilometer across at the widest part, and four hundred meters at the narrowest, was kidney shaped. In June, as in all the wooded areas in the region, its trees were in full leaf, and except for one or two long narrow cuttings in the southern end and a small

In places the forest was almost impenetrable. Observation was limited to a few feet—point-blank range. The German defense included mutually supporting machine guns—one protected the other—and infantry to keep the Marines at bay. Belleau Wood represented the perfect defense. *Marine Corps History Division*

The stone hunting lodge stood in the northern tip of the wood. Hundreds died before it and the surrounding forest were in Marine hands. The shattered ruins of the lodge stands today as a memorial to the dead of both sides. *Marine Corps History Division*

clearing in the northern third, it was very much in a state of nature.

Tall hardwood trees grow thickly in it, and under the trees it was choked with heavy underbrush and second growth. There was a small stone house called the Pavillon in the preserve; one narrow, unimproved road; and a few winding footpaths through the rest of it. There was a deep ravine in the southern edge and another deep ravine cut almost across it, angling northeast and southwest from the western edge, a little below its northern third. Within the woods there was a surprising variety of contour; knolls rose abruptly and great boulders thrust up from the ground. An outcropping of these gray, enormous stones—leprous with moss and frost-split—crowned the height in the southern face of the wood, offering natural protection from shellfire and an ideal location for machine guns.

Second Lieutenant William A. Eddy, 6th Marines intelligence officer, and his two scouts lay concealed in the uncut field, heavy with the smell of clover, just a few feet from a gravel road. The crunch of hobnail boots, guttural commands, and the muffled sound of engineer tools drowned out the night sounds. The three interlopers had heard enough and silently withdrew into the night. They reported, "The Germans are organizing in the woods and consolidating their machine-gun positions."

Except for Eddy's brief foray, the Marine Brigade was going into the attack with precious little intelligence. Patrols were ordered out, nevertheless.

Do You Want to Live Forever?

Gunnery Sergeant Daniel Joseph Daly, before becoming one of the most quoted Marines in history, was already one of only two Marines to have received the Medal of Honor—and he had two of them. During the China Relief Expedition, Daly was awarded the Medal of Honor for "distinguishing himself in the presence of the enemy at the battle of Peking, 14 August 1900."

He received the second while serving with the 15th Company. "Gunnery Sergeant Daly was one of the company to leave Port Liberte, Haiti, for a six-day reconnaissance. After dark on the evening of October 24, 1915, while crossing the river in a deep ravine, the detachment was suddenly fired upon from three sides by about four hundred Cacos [Haitian bandits] concealed in bushes about one hundred yards from the fort. The Marine detachment fought its way forward to a good position, which it maintained during the night, even although subjected to a continuous fire from the Cacos. At daybreak the Marines, in three squads, advanced in three different directions, surprising and scattering the Cacos in all directions. Gunnery Sergeant Daly fought with exceptional gallantry against heavy odds throughout this action."

Then came Belleau Wood, June 5, 1918. The *Chicago Daily Tribune*'s flamboyant war correspondent Floyd Gibbons wrote, "The oats and wheat in the open field were waving and snapping off—not from the wind but from rifle and machine-gun fire of German veterans in their well-concealed positions. . . . [Daly] swung his bayoneted rifle over his head with a forward sweep. He yelled at his men: 'Come on, you sons-of-bitches. Do you want to live forever?'"

Daly insisted that he had really exclaimed, "For Christ's sake, men, come on! Do you want to live forever?"

Sergeant Major Daniel Joseph Daly was well known for his humility. He refused the limelight, although he was one of the Corps' most heavily decorated enlisted men. In addition to the two Medals of Honor, he was awarded the Distinguished Service Cross, the French Medaille Militaire, and the Croix de Guerre. *Marine Corps History Division*

"Little or no reconnaissance or scouting appears to have been done," according to Brigadier General Harbord. "This was probably due to inexperience. In addition, maps were scarce, almost unobtainable, and the hachures [contour lines] gave no real information as to the physical features of the ground."

According to Marine historian Robert Debs Heinl, "The Bois de Belleau was a carefully organized center of resistance held by the 461st Imperial German Infantry, more than 1,200 men strong—the largest single body of combat-seasoned regular troops which Marines had confronted since Bladensburg."

Regarding Maj. Josef Bischoff, the German commander, John Thomason wrote, "Major Bischoff was an old West African soldier who had learned the art of bush-fighting in the German colonies. His infantry positions everywhere [were] stiffened by machine guns and *minenwerrfers* [large mortars], and his dispositions took full advantage of the great natural defensive strength of the woods." The forty-six-year-old major pushed his men to perform prodigies of labor in three days, turning Belleau Wood into "one huge machine-gun nest," containing nearly two hundred of the weapons. It would take nearly a month of desperate fighting and six separate attacks before the Marine Brigade finally cleared the woods. Asprey noted that Bischoff would later be awarded Germany's highest decoration for his defense of the woods.

The undergrowth allowed the Germans to conceal themselves until the Americans were within point-blank range. Thick vegetation also prevented communication among units, forcing small units to operate without support.
Marine Corps History Division

Most of the German positions were constructed of earthen machine-gun pits reinforced by logs. However, this photo clearly shows a concrete position, which would make it almost impervious to anything but direct infantry assault.
Marine Corps History Division

Berry's battalion assaulted across this wheat field toward the northeast into Belleau Wood. They were assailed by a perfect storm of machine-gun and rifle fire. *Marine Corps History Division*

Only a Few Men Returned

A motorcycle roared up to the 5th Marines PC in a swirl of dust. The passenger jumped out of the sidecar and rushed into the building, barely acknowledging the rifle salute of the two Marine sentries. He was immediately escorted to a large, well-appointed room that served as the regimental commander's office. With the barest of formalities, the messenger, Lt. Fielding Robinson of Harbord's staff, briefed Colonel Neville on the contents of Marine Brigade Field Order No. 2. In it, Neville's 3rd Battalion (Maj. Benjamin S. "Ben" Berry), less one company, was to attack straight east against the northern mass of Belleau Wood, while the 3rd Battalion, 6th Marines (Maj. Berton W. Sibley) was to seize the southern lobe of the wood. Neville asked about artillery support and was told that it was not planned because there was no need for it.

An observer from the French Escadron 252 (aircraft squadron) had earlier reported "sector calm." With that, the messenger strode out of the room to the waiting motorcycle and roared off to brief Colonel Catlin, 6th Marines.

As the Marines waited for the signal, one wrote, "The captain came along with a rifle swung across his shoulder and bayonet fixed. He said, 'Five minutes more; get all the rest you can.' I lay down in the wet grass and said a prayer. Then the word came, 'One minute; get ready.' "

"Forward!" A 2nd Division unpublished report stated, "At 5:00 p.m., the officers' whistles shrilled, and the two battalions of Marines went forward. The sun was low behind them, their lines were carefully dressed in the four-wave platoon formation taught by the French, and their shadows lay long and level on the wheat in front of them."

Looking northeast at the Bois de Belleau, over which Maj. Benjamin S. Berry's 1st Battalion, 5th Marines, made its ill-fated attack. *Marine Corps History Division*

The dashing, reckless *Chicago Tribune* correspondent Floyd Gibbons received permission from Neville to accompany the attack—"Go wherever you like, but I want to tell you it's damn hot up there." Gibbons linked up with battalion commander Ben Berry and started across the field, "which was perfectly flat and was covered with a young crop of oats between ten and fifteen inches high. The field was bordered on all sides by dense clusters of trees. In the trees . . . were German machine guns. And then it began to come hot and fast. Perfectly withering volleys of lead swept the tops of the oats just over us."

Almost immediately Gibbons heard a shout. "It came from Major Berry. 'My hand's gone,' he shouted. A ball had entered his left arm at the elbow, had traveled down the side of the bone, tearing away muscles and nerves of the forearm, and lodging in the palm of his hand. His pain was excruciating." Gibbons crawled over to help. Suddenly, he felt a burning sensation in his left arm and another in his left shoulder—two machine-gun bullets had hit him in less time then it takes to tell the tale. "Then there came a crash. It sounded like someone had dropped a glass bottle into a porcelain bathtub. It seemed that everything in the world turned white." A bullet had ricocheted off the ground, tore through his left eye and out his forehead, leaving him near death. The word went out that he had been killed.

Before the attack, Gibbons had sent a skeleton dispatch to the Paris censor, an old friend. When the censor heard that his friend had been killed, he released the dispatch unedited. "This is the last thing I can ever do for poor old Floyd." Gibbons story opened with, "I am up front and entering Belleau Woods with the U.S. Marines." Newspapers in the United States picked it up. The *New York Times* trumpeted, "Our Marines attack, gain mile at Veuilly, resume drive at night, foe losing heavily." And the *Chicago Daily Tribune* banner fairly screamed, "Marines Win Hot Battle Sweep Enemy From Height Near Thierry." The accounts were the first that mentioned specific units of the AEF by name, and they made it appear that the Marines were winning the war all by themselves.

The army was not amused and was convinced that the Leathernecks were a corps of publicity hounds. Maj. Gen. Robert L. Bullard, U.S. Army, wrote sarcastically, "The press reports of the 2nd

Floyd Gibbon's helmet clearly showing where the bullet penetrated the steel. *Floyd Gibbons,* And They Thought We Wouldn't Fight

Division's fight shouted, 'Marines, Marines, Marines' until the word resounded over the whole earth and made the inhabitants thereof, except for a few Americans in the Army in France, believe there was nothing in the 2nd Division and, indeed, nothing in front of the Germans, but Marines." He went on to write, "General Pershing came to visit me. 'General,' I said to him at dinner, 'I see that the 2nd Marines (emphasizing the 2nd as though the division was all Marines) have won the war at Belleau Wood.' 'Yes,' he answered dryly, 'and I stopped it yesterday as I passed there.'" Harbord was upset by the snide comments of his army contemporaries, "The Marines have been taunted . . . by some unkind and unjust comments from Army officers of high enough rank to be above such pettiness."

The German machine guns hammered away at the exposed Marines. Thomason wrote, "The sergeant beside the lieutenant stopped, looked at him with a frozen, foolish smile, and crumpled into a heap of old clothes. Something took the kneecap off the lieutenant's right knee and his leg buckled under him. He noticed, as he fell sideways, that all his men were tumbling over like duck-pins; there was one fellow that spun around twice, and went over backward with his arms up. Then the wheat shut him in, and he heard cries and a moaning."

Alfred Noble remembered, "You go down and nobody sees you go down, and it's a helpless feeling: you say 'If I get hit I am likely to stay hit, right here.' That was the trouble about wheat—people just disappeared in it, and were not found until they had bled to death."

Hospital Corpsmen

Pharmacist's Mate Second Class Frank Welte was attached to the 20th Company when it went "over the top." Within minutes he was swamped with casualties. "Welte dressed four wounded Marines, calmly writing their [wound] tags, and had started on the fifth man when he was struck in the back and right heel, while kneeling over his patient. Fragments of a bursting high-explosive shell painfully wounded him. He continued dressing his patient and filled in the diagnosis tag when his head was pierced by a machine-gun bullet. He gave his book of diagnosis tags to his patient, asking him to 'turn them over to the chief' when he arrived at the battalion [aid] station. With the delivery of the tags to the patient, Welte died."

At Belleau Wood, an aid station was established at the command post of each company, often in the center of the line, with the commander. An advanced aid station was set up about one hundred yards in

Regimental Chief Pharmacist Mate George C. Strott and Pharmacist Mate Leon H. French in front of the regimental aid station near Belleau Wood. The U.S. Navy furnished all medical support for the Marine brigade. A close bond of comradeship existed between the two services. *Marine Corps History Division*

the rear of the frontline, while battalion dressing stations were located about half a kilometer in the rear. Litter bearers, often men from the regimental bands, were designated to carry nonambulatory casualties from one aid station to the next, until they reached a point where motorized ambulances could be used. On average, it took about two hours to evacuate a man through the various stations until he reached a field hospital and more thorough treatment.

John West recalled the "cries of the wounded, 'first aid,' 'stretcher bearer,' pitiful pleading cries, cursing, pleading demands, 'Christ, Christ, Oh, God.' Wounded men pleaded with me to kill them to put them out of their misery, God, what a [day]."

Vic Bleasdale watched as the bullets "knocked down the men from the first two lines. They'd knock a man down and the goddamn bullets . . . would roll his body, and bullets would tear tufts of wool out of their uniforms. Of course, the man was dead—riddled, you know, with bands of fire; they couldn't help but be dead. We hadn't gotten across the damn field before the first line, the survivors, had merged with the second. The walking wounded headed for the rear. I didn't permit anybody to give them first aid, because if you let men help them, you have got that many less men. You can't stop in the middle of a goddamn attack for wounded men or anybody. You had to keep them in the line attacking. I know this is harsh but combat is no place for the weak."

Berry's three companies faced the western edge of the wood, which curved like the inner line of a

crescent. Hill 169 dominated the left flank of the battalion. There was no cover in the open wheat field, four hundred yards or more wide, and they were quickly shot to pieces, ending the attack almost before it had begun. Within an hour of going over the top, a severely wounded Berry sent a message to Harbord. "What is left of battalion is in woods close by. Do not know whether will be able to stand or not. Increase artillery fire."

His adjutant clarified the losses: "Three platoons of the 45th Company went over. Only a few [men] returned." In all, Berry's battalion suffered 4 officers and 268 men killed or wounded. It was now up to Sibley's 3rd Battalion, 6th Marines, to take the woods.

Sibley's battalion rushed into position to meet the attack schedule. There was "no time to reconnoiter the area and no maps. The company commanders hurried forward to have a quick look at the terrain they would be going over and through." At 5:00 p.m., the shrill notes of officers' whistles sounded along the battalion front. A thousand Marines deployed into formation in a

A squad of Marines lies together in death. The ranks of Marines advancing through the wheat were a machine gunner's dream. Dozens of Americans were cut down, and many were hit again as German grazing fire swept the open field. Lucky was the wounded man who found cover in a furrow or fold in the ground. *Marine Corps History Division*

Major Berton W. Sibley always led by example at the forefront of his men. Twice cited in general orders, he was awarded the Navy Cross and the Croix de Guerre with Palm for bravery in action. *Marine Corps History Division*

two-company front about nine hundred meters wide. The 82nd Company was on the left, 84th Company on the right, with the 83rd and 97th in support. The regimental commander watched as the ranks moved into the open fields. "It was one of the most beautiful sights I have ever witnessed," Colonel Catlin proudly recalled. "The battalion pivoted on its right, the left sweeping across the open ground in four waves, as steadily and correctly as though on parade; the men placed five yards apart and the waves fifteen to twenty yards behind each other. There was no yell and wild rush, but a deliberate forward march, with lines at right dress."

The two left flank companies advanced quickly through the southwestern end of the woods against light opposition and gained a height that was unoccupied. The thick scrub growth broke up the formations. Small groups of Marines led by an NCO or junior officer continued the attack. Suddenly, they ran into the main German defensive line and were stopped cold. Platoon commander Lt. Louis S. Timmerman found himself with only half the men he started out with. "Immediately a terrible fire from the left flank was opened up from a little rise of ground about fifty yards away, also from out left rear by machine guns . . . at this moment I was hit in the left side of the face and fell forward thinking, 'I've got mine,' as I thought

Officers and NCOs were shot down, yet the Marine assault continued, led by the bravest of the brave. They attacked through the forest, closing with the enemy hand to hand. *Marine Corps History Division*

a bullet had ripped through under my eye. It knocked me out for a minute, and then I felt better and although I was covered with blood I realized I had not been dangerously hit. My men were dropping all around, so I told them to follow me and we ran back to shelter."

The two right flank companies had hardly started when they were assaulted with a murderous barrage of machine-gun, mortar, and artillery fire and driven to ground. They had run into Major Bischoff's entrenched 461st Regiment. Private W. H. Smith saw "German machine guns everywhere, in the trees and in small ground holes, and camouflaged at other places so they couldn't be spotted . . . every blamed tree must have had a machine gunner." Sibley's Marines tried to advance across the killing fields. "My God, we tried," Pvt. Bob Benedict agonized, "but the machine guns were just too much. They just cut us to pieces." Stymied by the ferocious fire, Sibley sent a message to Harbord. "They are too strong for us. The losses are so heavy that I am reforming on the ground held by the 82nd Company last night. All of the officers of the 82nd Company [are] wounded or missing, and it is necessary to reform before we can advance. Machine guns too strong for us."

By the end of the day, four of the Marine Brigade's six battalions had been in action; Turrill's successful morning attack had advanced the brigade's lines

A portion of the German support line fronting Belleau Wood. The 461st Infantry Regiment under its commander Major Bischoff had prepared a defense in depth that would bleed the Marine Brigade white in a vicious no-holds-barred bloodbath. *Marine Corps History Division*

more than a thousand meters to Hill 142; Berry's evening attack against Belleau Wood had been a complete failure. His battered remnants had pulled back to their old positions, where they were reorganizing; Sibley had gained a toehold in the south face of the wood but at a severe cost—5 officers and 194 men; Holcomb's 2nd Battalion, 6th Marines, on the right, was under heavy German pressure in Bouresches. They had beaten off several counterattacks but the situation was dicey at best. Throughout the day, sketchy reports filtered back to brigade headquarters. It wasn't until early the

next morning that the full extent of the day's operation was known. The losses were staggering. More Marines had been killed and wounded in action than in the 143 years of the Corps' history. Total losses were 31 officers and 1,056 men, of which 6 officers and 222 men were killed or died of wounds. Harbord forwarded an operations report admitting serious difficulties, "The brigade can hold its present position but is not able to advance at present." Paradis listened to an officer recite the names of all the killed and wounded in his unit. "I couldn't see his face because it was so dark but I feel I could hear his tears."

German losses in the 237th Division were 5 officers and 48 men killed; 7 officers and 348 men wounded; and 1 officer and 72 men missing. The 10th Division lost 24 killed, 101 wounded, and 26 missing.

The Germans Are on Your Right

Fritz Wise had been in great form as he led his battalion through the dark night. He was mad as hell—"literally chewing the bark off the trees," according to Lieutenant Cooke—because he was supposed to establish contact with the 5th Marines headquarters to get orders. "Finding it would be a miracle. The night was black as pitch—impossible to see even one foot ahead." The men had to hold on to the man in front of him to keep from getting lost. They advanced about half a mile between two high banks when the terrain opened up into sloping grain fields with Belleau Wood on their right flank. "It was still as a graveyard when we started," Wise recalled. "Too damned peaceful, I told myself." He stopped the column and cautiously advanced a platoon from the 55th Company another two hundred yards. "Suddenly rifle fire broke out on our left. We could see flashes in the dark. A couple of my men dropped." Wise thought the rifles sounded like .03 Springfields and called out, "What the hell do you mean shooting into us! We're Americans." The shooting stopped immediately—it was the survivors from the 3rd Battalion. "Look out," they warned. "The Germans are on your right."

Wise immediately ordered his men back. "About face to the rear—on the double!" They hadn't gone twenty yards when suddenly machine-gun fire erupted, scything through the wheat. German mortars soon found the range and added a deadly barrage, blanketing the field with shards of jagged metal. Captain John Blanchfield,

Stylized drawing of Cpl. Paul Bonner's futile rescue of Capt. John Blanchfield. *Morgan Dennis,* Dear Folks at Home

the commander of the 55th Company, was near the front of the column. Wise "saw him grab at his groin and double over." Corporal Paul Bonner was close by. "I saw Blanchfield fall, right on the road. Everybody scattered. I started to run, then I thought of Blanchfield and I started back. Machine-gun bullets whipped across the road as I rushed across. I made it to the captain's side, picked him up, and carried him into the woods where a doctor started treatment." It was too late; he died within minutes. Before the battle, Blanchfield had had a premonition of his death, which he had related to Lem Shepherd.

Lieutenants Cooke and Shepherd were near the rear of the company. "We picked up our feet and galloped back in the direction from which we came." Shepherd led his platoon to the left, along the edge of the woods. He heard someone frantically shout out, "Captain Blanchfield's been wounded, you're to take command!"

"I carried on getting the platoons in position along the edge of the woods. Fire was coming from the little woods to my front and also from Belleau Wood on the right." The young officer and his orderly dashed from cover to cover along the edge of the woods to the PC. Rifle and machine-gun bullets snapped overhead. Mortar and artillery rounds exploded, shaking the ground with tremendous concussions. Suddenly, the orderly cried out and went down, a Mauser slug in his leg. Shepherd bent down to help the Marine when something walloped him in the left thigh, "like the kick of a mule. I crumpled in a heap, unable to move, not realizing that I had been hit. I glanced down and what should I see on the ground beside me but the bullet which had struck me." Blood was oozing from his trousers. His little pet dog KiKi, who had loyally followed, was on the ground beside him, his head on Shepherd's leg. He was so quiet Shepherd thought he was dead: " 'Damn it, they shot little KiKi too,' and I picked him up and threw him off me, but he jumped up and ran right back to me. I was elated, 'My God, my dog's safe.' " The two wounded men lay in the road until a Marine from Shepherd's platoon dragged them to safety.

The battalion deployed on a ridge facing Belleau Wood. According to Wise the Germans pounded the position with "a continuous shelling with all the artillery in range, and poured in an unceasing stream of machine-gun and rifle fire. Everywhere up and down the line, masses of earth, chunks of rock, splinters of trees, leaped into the air as the shells exploded. Machine-gun and rifle bullets thudded into the earth unendingly." German trench mortars in the woods opened up. "Those aerial torpedoes, nearly four feet long, packed with TNT," Wise explained, "would come sailing through the air and land on the ridge. That earth literally shook every time one of them exploded."

Lieutenant Cooke had just climbed out of his PC. "The hot blast of a heavy shell blew me right back in again. Another shell lifted the cover of my shelter and set it down again, showering me with dirt and broken bricks. Machine-gun bullets hammered through the trees above, cutting down whole limbs at a time. The Heinies [Germans] had me spotted!"

The battalion absorbed tremendous punishment for the next three days. Lieutenant W. H. Matthews, the intelligence officer, estimated one in four men became casualties.

"Marines at Belleau Wood: U.S. Marines cleaning out machine-gun nests in Belleau Wood."
Frank E. Schoonover–National Museum of the Marine Corps

Chapter 8

Belleau Wood

Lieutenant E. D. Cooke groped his way into the darkened farmhouse. "Colonel Neville and Colonel Wise were hunched over a map spread out on a table. Blankets covered the windows and the flame of a single candle jumped and quivered as the air was fanned by nearby guns. In the darkened corners sat Murray, Dunbeck, Williams, and several other company officers. 'Gentlemen,' said Colonel Wise, 'tomorrow we take the Bois de Belleau."

Wise was directed to attack east across the open ground, then once in the woods, pivot north. In the confusion of the fighting, his battalion fought to the eastern edge of the woods, thinking they had captured the entire objective. *G. Kelly Fitch, featured in* At Belleau Wood, *by Robert B. Asprey*

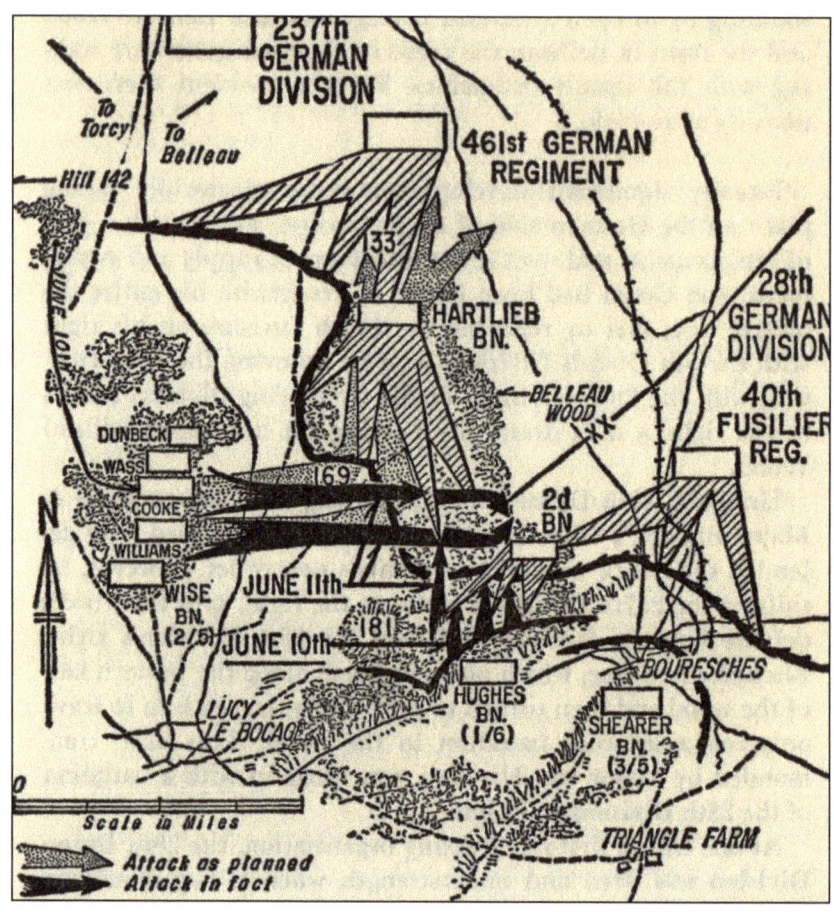

Wise received orders to take his battalion along the Lucy–Torcy road toward Belleau Wood. "A runner showed up, asking for me. 'A message, sir,' he said, when I called for him. I looked at my wrist watch—midnight. I unfolded the message he handed me, crouched down, and turned the light of my electric torch on the paper. I couldn't believe my eyes; it was an attack order!" Private Schiani was close enough to see Wise in the dim light. "Colonel Wise had a beard now, and smoking a stub of a cigarette, he looked tired, as we all did by now. I can never forget that scene of desperation as events began to unfold."

Wise's battalion was ordered to attack from the southern edge of the woods, into the teeth of the German defenses. "I was dumbfounded," Wise recalled dejectedly. "It meant the needless death of most of my battalion." At 3:30 a.m. American heavy artillery opened fire on the front line of the German 461st Infantry Regiment.

"A hurricane of steel lashed and tore at the borders of the wood," Lieutenant Cooke related.

"The worst night of my life," an entry in a German diary noted.

After the battle, a Marine points to the southern edge of Belleau Wood where Wise's battalion attacked across open ground. *Marine Corps History Division*

"I am lying in a thick woods on an open height in little holes behind rocks, for this is certainly heavy artillery fire."

Sergeant Curtis Bevington, U.S. Marines, wrote that the area "is shell-torn and hardly a tree has its complete set of limbs. Shrapnel has torn away most of the leaves." The violent bombardment, however, not only failed to destroy the enemy, it gave them a warning. "They knew from the barrage that the attack was coming," Wise related. "I stood there under some trees by a ditch on the southern edge of the Bois de Belleau . . . in the growing light." A heavy mist lay in the low ground, offering some cover for the men as they formed for the assault. "I watched my battalion march into position."

According to an unpublished 2nd Division account, "The weight of the German defense lay southward, exactly where the Marine attack struck the German lines." The Marines were about to attack into a buzz saw. The Germans had cleverly positioned light machine guns to cover every path and clearing. Heavy machine guns, protected by swarms of infantry, backed them up, creating a near perfect defense.

Wise debated on two courses of action for assaulting the woods; an encircling maneuver and a straight frontal attack. His officers debated back and forth, until Wise lost patience. He pointed to Lieutenant Cooke and demanded, "Have you seen any Germans in those woods?" Cooke admitted that he had not seen any. "Of course not," Wise shouted, "there probably aren't any Boche in those woods at all. That means we will simply have to walk over and take the place." Wise was supported by the French, who told the Americans that the woods were not strongly held and ordered them to attack. "As soon as possible, the American 2nd Division will seize the Bois de Belleau and the long crest, which immediately dominates Torcy and Belleau."

Captain Wass looked at the luminous dial on his wristwatch. "Four thirty," he announced, in a tight, hard voice. "The whistles of our platoon leaders sounded up and down the line," Wise nostalgically recalled. "The battalion rose to its feet. Bayonets fixed, rifles at the ready, the men started their slow advance." Cooke watched the first two companies move forward into the thick mist. "Some light Maxims had gotten inside our barrage

Artillery stripped the foliage from the trees, leaving jagged stumps looking like dead fingers pointing skyward. The broken branches littered the ground. The Germans cunningly integrated the debris into their defense positions. *Marine Corps History Division*

zone and opened fire. Our forward lines stumbled for a moment, then moved into the tall wheat, through a fence, and clear of the grain. The ground [was] torn and ripped into deep holes by the barrage that crept just ahead of our assault." The forest loomed ahead, dark and foreboding. "Without the slightest warning those shadows suddenly were split apart by chattering, stabbing flames. A crackling sheath of machine-gun bullets encased our battalion, closing in on us fiercely."

Shattered remnants of barbed wire littered the ground, ready to snag the unwary attacker and hold him until a bullet ended his advance. *Marine Corps History Division*

The Marines in the foreground are firing rifle grenades into the woods, while others in the background provide covering fire for the two men advancing on the right. The white smoke is probably from a white phosphorous shell. *Marine Corps History Division*

Wise stared helplessly as the German gunners ranged in on the advancing Marines—"men dropping, men dropping, men dropping." Cooke shouted, "Down! Down, take cover!" "Some were already down—down to stay. Many hurled themselves into the nearest shell hole, but a few of those kids stubbornly pushed forward until their legs were shot out from under them." Sergeant Jerry Thomas watched the attack. "I climbed a slope, saw Wise and his command group in a wheat field ahead. On his left and slightly forward the attacking waves were moving through the wheat, the men falling right and left. I didn't know what was happening, except that Wise was getting the hell shot out of him."

In some spots a line of dead men marked a traversing Maxim. Cooke peered over the edge of a shell hole where he had sought cover. "I saw one of my connecting files stretched close to earth in a furrow of ground. I crawled forward and shook his leg. The man was dead. To one side lay another, doubled up, both arms locked rigidly about his shattered middle. Off to the left a gun rattled and bullets searched the air a bare few inches above my cowering body. When the gun ceased I lifted my head and saw a third man crawling towards me, painfully dragging his right leg. It was Lieutenant Cummings of the 51st Company and his ankle was smashed. 'Where's your outfit?' I asked. 'The machine guns got 'em. As far as I know I'm the only one left out of ten officers and two hundred and

fifty men." Before contact was lost with the 1st Company of the German 461st Regiment, it reported fifty dead Americans in front of their lines.

Private F. E. Steck, 51st Company, was one of the "fortunate" ones who were only wounded; he survived. "I was in the front when three machine-gun bullets got me. One went into the neck, another in my left shoulder, and the third in my arm. I took cover in a shell hole until a Marine found me and dragged me to a first-aid dugout." Another Marine from his company "spotted a machine gun. Without a thought we charged it. Two were killed immediately and I was shot in the right leg but the rest surrounded the gun crew, who wanted to surrender. There's not much use taking as prisoners men who fire at you until they see they are overpowered. I don't remember any prisoners walking back from that crowd."

Lieutenant Cooke had finally had enough. "Duty, responsibility, and something like rage took command of my thoughts. I actually shucked off fear like an old coat. I stood up in plain sight and blew a blast on my whistle. From holes, furrows, and clods of dirt, faces looked up. I pointed at the woods to our right front—and walked forward. About twenty men were right behind me, and more came running, eager to do anything that was wanted."

"Yard by yard they advanced," Wise recalled proudly. "I saw them disappear into the woods."

Private William Francis made it into the trees

Two German soldiers amid the debris of combat. A "potato masher" grenade lies on the ground just in front of the first soldier's helmet. *Marine Corps History Division*

but was singled out by a German machine gunner and a sniper. "I saw a little rock in front of me that would afford a little protection so I made for this. It was only high enough to protect my head. My light pack was riddled with bullets, rock chips peppered my face, and bark was clipped off a little tree that stood six inches from my head." A friend was hit just in front of him. "He was hit in the side and bleeding badly. Every time I would make a move the Germans would try for me again. I was pinned down and had to play dead, even though my friend was bleeding to death. There was nothing I could do." The profane Vic Bleasdale said the "Germans had some splendid snipers. Those sons-of-bitches seldom missed. They killed a guy I was

talking to. I was leaning over, talking to him when the sniper shot him right in the face."

Wise could hear the sounds of fighting. "The detonations of the barrage had ceased. A sudden ripping burst of machine-gun fire would break out. That meant the Marines were advancing on a nest. It would die down. That meant that the nest was taken. I came upon one of those machine guns camouflaged behind a brush pile. Dead Marines lay in front of it. Dead Germans lay about it. The youngster in command [Marine NCO] told me of the terrific fighting they'd had. Foot by foot they had pushed their way through the underbrush in the face of continuous machine-gun and rifle fire. Snipers had shot them from brush piles on the ground; from perches high in the trees. Germans they had left sprawled on the ground for dead had risen and shot them in the back."

Private Lewis A. Holmes, 49th Company, "lost all sense of feeling for any German." He saw one, who was pretending to be dead, take "two shots at a wounded Marine and kill him. Well, the kid with me jumped up and ran to the German and gave him a 'good ole American bayonet' for his punishment. He won't shoot another American."

A wounded corporal, Willard P. Nelligan, was making his way to a dressing station when his "eyes were opened to the brutalities of the Germans." "As the wounded were being carried back they had to pass an open space. The Germans had a machine-gun sniper picking off the wounded."

Merwin Silverthorn expressed his feelings in a letter to his father. "If you have had your pals killed alongside of you, and have missed death

The cost of war. German soldiers lying where they have fallen. *Marine Corps History Division*

The close hand-to-hand combat often precluded taking prisoners. It was a kill-or-be-killed, shoot-first bloodletting. *Morgan Dennis,* Dear Folks at Home

yourself a number of times, by inches, are you going to have mercy on the coward that shoots wounded men—would you have mercy? This is the time for the bayonet."

As Wise carefully worked his way through the trees, he ran into a disheveled Captain Wass— "one legging was gone, the other dragging, and his blouse was torn half off him, but he still had on his Sam Browne and every Dutchman in the place was trying to get him because he was an officer." Wass told him of "the difficulties they had in orienting themselves in the heavy underbrush. There were no landmarks, once you got into those woods. If you turned around twice you lost all sense of direction and only your compass could straighten you out." Wise continued on down the line and found the exhausted commander of the 55th Company. The frustrated officer told him, "Whenever we took a machine-gun nest, another one opened up from the flank. That happened many times. The second one would never fire a shot until we had taken the first. Then they opened up on us."

Less than two hours after starting the attack, the exhausted survivors went to ground to reorganize and count noses. "It was bad news," Lieutenant Cooke reported. "Wass had about a third of his men . . . sixteen men were all that was left of the 51st Company [its commander, Lloyd 'Retreat Hell' Williams, was killed]. . . . Milner commanded remnants of the 43rd . . . [and] I had eighty men . . . a bitter price to pay for a piece of woods that stank of high explosive, crushed shrubbery, and shattered human flesh. Dead men littered the ground and lay hidden in every thicket and rocky cleft. Even the living walked about in a sort of shell-shocked daze." The Germans had also suffered

Two Marines sit in a large foxhole in the shattered remains of Belleau Wood after the battle. The photo clearly shows the effects of the battle and the difficulty in knowing one's position. *Marine Corps History Division*

Marines visit their fallen buddies after the battle. *Marine Corps History Division*

After days of combat and no food, except for emergency rations, the surviving Marines were totally exhausted.
Marine Corps History Division

Worn-out survivors were low on morale, having seen hundreds of their fellow soldiers killed. *Marine Corps History Division*

A Marine foxhole during a quiet moment in Belleau Wood. The Marine has spread out his mess gear on the ground at the edge of the foxhole. *Marine Corps History Division*

Shattered trees among the huge boulders that provided the defenders with excellent defensive positions. *Marine Corps History Division*

heavily. The 1st and 4th companies of the 461st Regiment were overrun and simply disappeared. Two other companies were forced out of position after suffering heavy casualties and retreated toward the northeast. A German soldier wrote, "My company has been reduced from 120 to 30 men . . . we have Americans opposite us who are terribly reckless fellows."

Wise reported to Harbord that "all objectives reached and we are consolidating," which was not

true; two-thirds of the woods lay to the north. His attack had gone straight across the southern edge of the woods and had reached the eastern edge, not the northeastern edge as ordered.

Asprey wrote that "Wise was completely in the dark as to the true location of his companies, not to mention their shot-up state."

Lieutenant William Matthews, the battalion intelligence officer tried to correct his intransigent commander. "You goddamn young bonehead,"

Wise shouted, "You don't know what you're talking about!" It would be another day before Harbord learned of the mistake, and in the meantime, he planned another attack, believing Belleau Wood was firmly in the hands of his brigade.

Dead Tired

The survivors of the attack, both German and American, were totally exhausted—physically and mentally. Each side dug in, often no more than a few yards separated the two antagonists. Private Malcolm Aitken "had no idea where we were so we decided to stay and defend ourselves as best we could. . . . I was so close to the Germans that I could hear them talk and work the bolts in their guns. I had my trench knife in one hand and my rifle in the other, waiting to be either killed or captured. I often wonder who was the more afraid—the Germans or I." Cooke put what was left of his company undercover, then he "quite shamelessly crawled under a projecting boulder and, despite the heavy presence of death, went to sleep."

Early the next morning, Harbord met with Wise and the regimental commanders. Harbord was under the impression that the Germans held only a small section in the northwestern edge of the woods. Wise was still in the dark and thought that "with some artillery preparation, he could

The fall of 1918 would bring the final offensive of the war, the Meuse-Argonne Offensive, also known as the Battle of the Argonne Forest. Here, a 37mm gun crew from Headquarters Company, 6th Marines, covers an advance through the dense, heavily-shelled forest, the same conditions they had faced in Belleau Wood, which lay less than a hundred miles to the east. *National Archives*

The stone Pavillon was the French landlord's hunting lodge. The area around it was heavily defended and had to be taken by the bayonet. *George Scott—Cold Steel, U.S. Marines First Hand Battle, eyewitness—The* Chicago Daily News *War Postal Card Department*

dislodge the Germans in the afternoon." Harbord agreed and ordered an hour of artillery preparation before the attack. Promptly at 4:00 a.m. the 12th Field Artillery Regiment opened fire, which was extended, after Wise requested another hour. Unknown to the Marines, the barrage turned out to be totally wasted; it landed north of the German positions and succeeded only in rearranging the forest. At 5:30 p.m., the battered Marines rose out of their holes and attacked straight north, three companies on line—55th, 43rd, and 18th in that order, with the 51st Company in reserve.

Cooke and his handful of exhausted survivors stepped forward. "We didn't want to make an attack. Hundreds of our men lay stiff in death already. A large part of our effectives were replacements. Reaction from the attack of the day before had left us low in morale and courage." Almost immediately they ran into intense German fire—in some cases, the lines were separated by only fifty feet. "The Boche heard us coming and gave us all they had," Cooke lamented. "Light machine guns camouflaged in trees, heavy guns on the

ground, grenades, rifles, pistols; everything was turned loose at once. A burst of bullets smashed into a man's jaw beside me, carrying away the lower part of his face. A grenade fell on the other side, tearing a youngster's legs to shreds."

Casualties mounted. Officers went down and "when sergeants fell, corporals picked up their commands; when they fell, privates took over." In the midst of the carnage, a Marine screamed "Eyah," the battle cry he had learned at boot camp. "The yell they had learned on the bayonet course, sticking dummies—and in that narrow neck of Belleau Wood it was taken up and shouted savagely," Cooke recalled emotionally. "The kids were startled by that yell. Fear, hunger, fatigue—everything seemed forgotten in a mad lust to ram two feet of steel into some Heinie's innards!" The attackers pressed forward, overrunning the enemy's advanced positions and breaking through their main line of heavy machine guns.

Cooke proudly recalled, "We crushed the Germans' forward line," as his men reached the edge of the woods near Hill 133. "In the field to our left, from where they had been working around our flank, a group of gray-clad figures got up like a covey of frightened quail—big, husky Huns, running over the ploughed ground with stilted awkwardness in their heavy boots. For a stupefied moment I stared with open mouth, then, clawing out my automatic, I let go an entire clip at their retreating backs. The whole company discharged a scattered volley—and we never hit a damn one!"

Lieutenant Drinkard B. "Drink" Milner, leading the remnants of the 43rd Company after its commander was wounded and evacuated, climbed up in the Pavillon where he could see Germans in the streets of Belleau. Moments later, a wounded, English-speaking German officer stepped out of the undergrowth and hailed the surprised Marine officer. A number of enemy soldiers watched from the woods. Milner's men trained their rifles on the newcomers in a tense standoff. Milner recovered quickly and offered the German a cigarette—wondering who was about to be captured. The German finally broke the silence by asking for a guide to take him and his men back to surrender. A greatly abashed Milner had to ask the German if he knew the way to the American lines—he didn't know the location of his own battalion. The slightly nonplussed German oriented Milner, signaled his men, and with a final wave started for the rear under a small detail of guards—forty-two men of the 461st Regiment followed him into captivity.

The Germans reported, "Gangs of men ten to twenty strong appeared in the rear of the 2nd Battalion, 40th Fusilier Regiment. Brave conduct . . . some of the wounded men carried on despite their injuries. Our men have thrown hand grenades into those clumps of men; enemy didn't pay any attention to them. Shoot while they walk, with their rifles under their arms. Carry no hand grenades, but use knives, pistols, rifle butts, and bayonets . . . big husky fellows, every one of them—rowdies—absolutely no military bearing."

Wass' 18th Company reached the northeastern edge, where Cooke saw "Sergeant Colvin scramble up the side of a rocky cliff after a machine gun, like a cat chasing birds on a tin roof. Still nearer was Wass, pursuing a frightened Heinie over a pile of cordwood." Wass finished his business and took stock of the situation. He realized that casualties had so thinned out the battalion that they could

German grenadier. *John W. Thomason Jr.,* Fix Bayonets!

not maintain their current position and ordered the survivors to "guide right," along the eastern edge of the woods.

As the Marines crabbed sideways to the right, the Germans took advantage of the situation and infiltrated into the vacated space to build up a new line of resistance. "There was a hole on our left that a regiment could walk through; and our own artillery didn't seem able to locate us and give support," Cooke related. "But our kids put the last clip of ammunition into their rifles and dared the Boche to come on." Wise notified Harbord, "[I] have one replacement officer per company left and about three hundred men, not including replacements." Three days previously, the battalion numbered thirty officers and one thousand men.

On watch, while the others huddle behind cover, trying to relax.
Col. Charles Waterhouse–National Museum of the Marine Corps

Chapter 9

Woods of the Marine Brigade

Sergeant Don Paradis delivered messages through the blood-drenched woods thick with the bodies of the fallen. "The stench of decayed bodies was nearly unbearable. Both dead Germans and Americans lay where they had fallen. Because of the warm days they deteriorated fast and flies hatched in open wounds, bottle flies, I mean. There was no one that could be spared for burial details." Vic Bleasdale remembered "one man—Jesus, his whole goddamn arm looked as if it was shot off—a horrible looking mess, but he was walking—he was holding himself—trying to get to the first-aid station."

Burial details searched the woods for the fallen of both sides. The soldiers were often buried where they were found, Allied and German graves existing side by side. *Marine Corps History Division*

A melancholy Pvt. Malcolm D. Aitken recalled, "We are in a little foxhole in reserve after the Belleau Woods and Bouresches fracas. Alas only a few are left of the gang. We buried scads of them in the hot sun for two days. They were bluish-black in color and the odor beggars description. It was a job and a half to get their dog tags and personal effects . . . took quite a time. After laying them side by side forty or so to a six-foot trench we stood with uncovered heads while the service, short and to the point, was recited. There were some twenty of us on the detail and we recognized several of our former friends. We had to go out with stretchers and pick them up . . . very carefully and roll them into the trench in a very careful manner after having been searched for personal effects. The one tag was left on the body, the other attached to a rude cross at the head. Our chaplain kept score in his little book, listing the effects under the name and address of the body where possible."

After surviving the hell of combat, the indefatigable Sergeant Paradis faced one more horror—"the sight of the rotting bodies of our boys." He led a burial party. "We cleared the brush and stone and wood from one side of the dead men and laid blankets out beside them. I fished out their dog tags . . . and took shovels and rolled the bodies onto the blankets. Some of the boys tried putting on their gas masks to overcome the stench; it made some of them vomit. We gathered in the sides and ends of the blanket and carried the body to the grave, sometimes dripping liquid on our clothing and shoes." After finishing, Paradis returned to his

Soldiers attend a ceremony at a large and well-organized American graveyard in the now-quiet woods. *Marine Corps History Division*

Bodies and equipment were strewn everywhere after the battle. These are the remains of some German machine gunners. *Marine Corps History Division*

Above: The grim work of grave digging. Taking care of the dead was a ghastly business; the summer heat quickened decomposition, and shellfire dismembered many of the bodies. *Marine Corps History Division*

Left: Remnants of Maj. Thomas Holcomb's battalion. At the start of the battle, the battalion numbered more than one thousand men. *Marine Corps History Division*

dugout. "As I dropped inside, a buddy shouted, 'For God's sake, get out of here, you're dead too.' I had human remains on my clothing."

Cooke was almost beyond caring. "Corpses lolling grotesquely in the dirt, no water, no food, ammunition almost gone, and the Germans were creeping closer. We lost the sense of emotion. Dull-eyed, resigned, lacking the courage to go forward or back, yet we clung desperately to that rocky edge of woods. It seemed to be all we had left in the world and we would not give it up. Not for Heinie, Kaiser Bill, nor the devil himself." On the 15th, the 2nd Battalion was relieved. It was just in time. "My nerves were completely shot. I cowered in a fox-hole at the sound of every shell and cringed at any unexpected noise," Cooke grimly recalled. "If a man suddenly yelled in my ear I'd have probably shot him dead."

Relief

Harbord was concerned about the poor condition of his men. The brigade had been in action for two weeks, with little sleep, no hot food—subsisting on iron rations—and little water. Heavy casualties—approaching 50 percent—had greatly reduced combat efficiency, which the untrained replacements had not been able to restore. In a report to the division commander, Harbord wrote, "Officers and men are at a state scarcely less than complete physical exhaustion. Men fall asleep under bombardment and the physical exhaustion and heavy losses are a combination calculated to damage morale, which should be met by immediate arrangements for the relief of this Brigade . . . in order to enable us to rest and reorganize."

Major General Omar Bundy, the division commander, concurred and requested the use of the U.S. 7th Infantry Regiment from the French corps commander. The 7th Infantry Regiment "belonged" to the French corps and they refused to release it. At that point, Bundy got his dander up and "threatened to exercise his seniority as ranking American officer present . . . to assume command of all American troops." The French, realizing there was a new tough guy in town, acquiesced. The 7th Infantry Regiment went into Belleau Wood on the evening of the 15th.

The battered remnants of the brigade turned over their positions. "My company, with some of the 43rd attached, filed silently back through the spectral forest and the ruins that had once been Lucy," Cooke recalled. "Stealthily we slipped past buildings that were tumbled to the ground, under beams reared on end, around shell holes gaping in the streets. Smoke eddied about our feet while gas clung to the broken walls and dripped from crevices. We kept no formation. Each man simply followed the one in front. No one was going to let himself be left behind. We wanted to hurry but our legs acted as though gripped by an undertow. Weak, starved, and apprehensive we bent forward, painfully propelling ourselves up the hill from Lucy, pathetically eager to escape . . . with each step we gained confidence and strength."

The battalion sent to relieve Wise was late. "Through the darkness before dawn I sat there in PC waiting for the 7th Infantry to show up. Day broke and they had not shown up. I was getting damn mad. It was a certainty they were going to get cut up, coming in by daylight. A couple of hours [later] their columns came in sight, marching across the open fields. I looked up. The German sausages [observation balloons] were there. I knew if they kept on . . . the German artillery would play hell with them. I ran across the field toward them, cursing. 'Don't you Goddamned fools know there's a war on? Get your men over into the ditch!' They followed up the ditch, and in its shelter got into the woods just in time. German shells were tearing the hell out of the open space where they had been five minutes before."

Wise watched his men leave Belleau Wood. "Two weeks growth of beard bristled on their faces. Deep lines showed, even beneath beard and dirt. Their eyes were red around the rims, bloodshot, burnt out. They were grimed with earth. Their cartridge belts were almost empty. They were damned near exhausted—past physical limits, traveling on their naked nerve." His battalion would not see Belleau Wood again, although they had paid a terrible price for the place. "I had left Courcelles May 31st with nine hundred and sixty-five men and twenty-six officers; now before me stood three hundred and fifty men and six officers. Some had fallen at Les Mares Farm; some in the bottleneck and on the ridge across from the Bois de Belleau. The most of them had gone down that morning we took the woods—dead or in hospitals far to the rear."

Woods Now
U.S. Marine Corps Entirely

The 7th Infantry held the line for the Marine Brigade from June 15 to June 24, enabling it to rest and recuperate. On the 23rd, Maj. Maurice E. Shearer's 3rd Battalion, 5th Marines, was ordered back into the fray, with orders to "clear the woods forthwith." At 5:00 p.m. sharp, Shearer's battalion went over the top and ran into the same buzz saw of German machine-gun positions. The 16th Company alone reported an "estimated sixteen heavy machine guns and thirty-five light type in their sector." The attack failed. The farthest advance was about twenty yards, which was immediately made untenable by intense machine-gun fire. "The enemy seems to have unlimited alternate gun positions and many guns," Shearer reported. "Each gun position covered by others. I know of no other way of attacking these positions with chance of success than one attempted and am of opinion that infantry alone cannot dislodge enemy guns."

Shearer's report had an effect. The next day, General Bundy met with Harbord and the brigade's regimental and battalion commanders. After a lengthy discussion, it was decided to pound the German positions with an overwhelming artillery bombardment. Harbord ordered that "the fire be intense enough . . . to prevent the entrance of any Germans. It will be the intention to follow

Major Maurice E. Shearer served in the Spanish-American War as an enlisted man in the army. He was commissioned a second lieutenant in the Marine Corps in 1905. He took command of the 3rd Battalion, 5th Marines, on June 15, 1918, and led it throughout the war. He received the Navy Distinguished Service Cross for "exceptionally meritorious service." *Marine Corps History Division*

up the artillery preparation by an attack with the 3rd Battalion. The rate of advance . . . will not exceed one hundred meters each three minutes."

From 3:00 a.m. until 5:00 p.m., fourteen hours straight, the 155mm howitzers of the 17th Field Artillery and the French 333rd concentrated on an area only six hundred meters square. Among the men scheduled to make the attack was a young twenty-year-old private named William A. Francis. "We learned that our artillery had orders to shell the woods with three- and six-inch guns for fourteen hours. We spent the morning and

seven hundred of us went over this time . . . all that was left of our battalion. We went over in a skirmish line, but had only gone a little distance when the Germans opened with two-pounders. They were hitting directly in our line, killing men right and left. They were coming so close that I could feel the stir of the air from them, and the boy on my left was hit in the side. Two of us dragged him behind a rock and left him for the first-aid man. A sergeant on my right was hit in the arm, but all he did was curse and go on. We had a wonderful barrage from our artillery, which was falling only a few yards in front of us, all the time we were advancing, keeping up with a creeping barrage."

early afternoon bringing up ammunition. The Germans sniped at us with one-pounders or whiz bangs, but we lost only one man from our detail. We got back just in time to go over the top."

At 5:00 p.m. the artillery lifted and Shearer's men attacked. "Heavy firing on us just before we jumped off," he reported. "Several casualties . . . very little machine-gun fire . . . will go through if humanly possible." William Francis "grabbed a piece of bread and took my place in the line. About

Two hours later Shearer sent another report. "47th Company gained objective—20th and 47th digging in . . . 45th still in reserve but will occupy positions as soon as things settle . . . 16th still working into position." Francis made it to the top of a little knoll. "The Germans opened up with

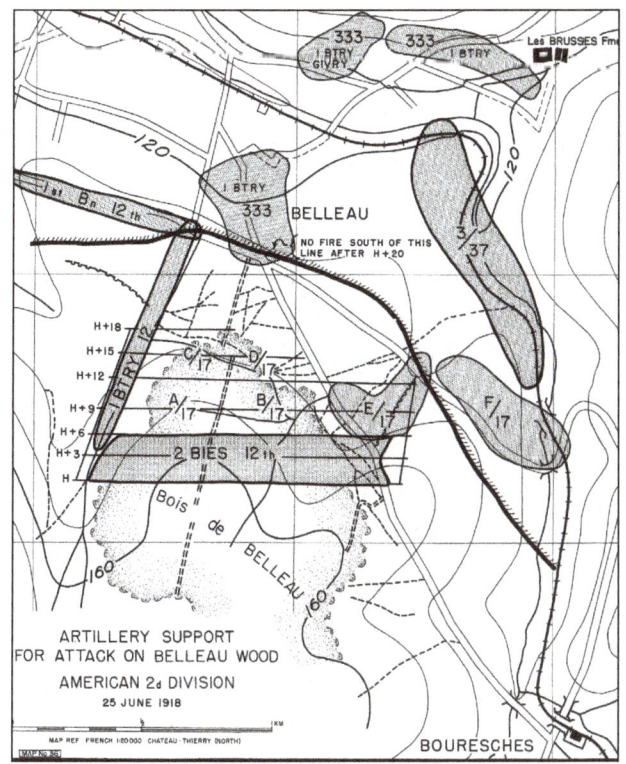

Left: The shelling blanketed German defenses, forcing them north. Marines followed behind the advancing bombardment, eliminating remaining Germans until Belleau Wood belonged to the Marines. *Northwest of Chateau Thierry: 1 June–10 July (unpublished 2nd Division report)* **Right:** Remnants of a German trench. Note the abandoned helmets, machine-gun ammunition, entrenching tool, and gas mask. Shattered planks mark the entrance to an underground dugout. *Marine Corps History Division*

"Kamerad." *John W. Thomason Jr.,* Fix Bayonets!

"A Kraut officer surrenders the hard way." *John W. Thomason Jr.,* Fix Bayonets!

machine guns, hand and rifle grenades, and trench mortars. Just then we all seemed to go crazy for we gave a yell like a bunch of wild Indians and started down the hill running and cursing in the face of the machine-gun fire. Men were falling on every side, but we kept going, yelling and firing as we went. I was the first man in the trench. I found a bunch of Germans in their dugout, and I ran

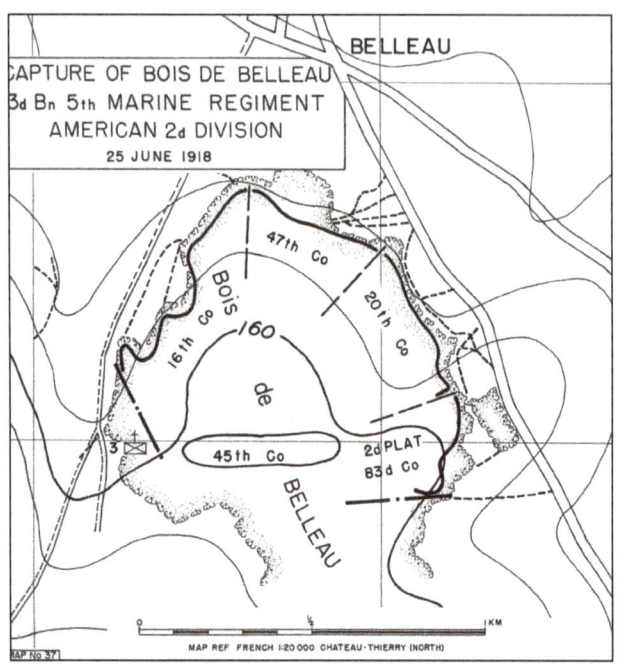

Disposition of Shearer's battalion after their successful attack on June 25. A fourteen-hour bombardment of the German positions softened them up for the final push. *Northwest of Chateau Thierry: 1 June–10 July (unpublished 2nd Division report)*

Frisking a German prisoner. *Marine Corps History Division*

them out. I often wonder why they didn't shoot me when I jumped into their trench; probably they were as afraid as I."

The fight continued well into the night. Shearer sent another message, "Seven prisoners, including one officer. The two left platoons of the 16th Company reporting grenades and sniper working on them." Shearer used the prisoners to carry his wounded to the rear, under guard from the more lightly wounded. He couldn't spare able-bodied men because of heavy casualties. At 8:20 p.m. he reported that the 47th Company was being counterattacked and needed artillery support. Two hours later he pleaded for reinforcements. "Any counterattack by enemy will be fatal to us in present condition. . . . We must not lose what we have now . . . had to use reserve company in line. . . . We have taken practically all of woods but do need help to clean it up and hold it."

Although Shearer's battalion had suffered a considerable number of casualties, the Germans had also been hit hard. The artillery bombardment had torn into their defenses, destroying many machine-gun positions and affecting morale.

Hundreds surrendered. A lost Marine runner wandered into a German position and was taken prisoner. He was confronted by an officer who asked him in excellent English if the attack was going to continue. The fast-thinking American replied that an entire regiment was coming at daylight. After a hurried conference with his officers, the German officer decided to surrender. The young Marine ordered them to lay down their arms, and then calmly led them back to his lines. "What will I do with these prisoners I have just captured?" he asked at the surprised outpost. The final count was four officers and seventy-eight men.

Hell Wood

Sergeant Daniel E. Morgan wrote that "the survivors of the fight in Belleau Woods never refer to it by any other name than Hell Wood. The unnumbered hordes of the poor German dead mingled with ours. I saw them hanging dead in the barbed wire, cuddled behind trees with head and shoulders stuck part way in the ground, fives, and tens, huddled in groups. Blood, flesh, blankets, shoes, rifles, canteens, were scattered everywhere: other lines or groups of men lying in rows with their picks and shovels, where they fell while digging for protection.

"I almost went mad before I got out of that wood."—Sgt. Daniel E. Morgan *Marine Corps History Division*

"The sun was burning hot. Those countless hordes of life-less forms were causing us no end of trouble. It became impossible for us to any longer stand the smell of the decomposed bodies. They had by this time all turned a sort of bluish-black. We tried to bury them. Two or three of us would get out and drag one or two of them to a shell hole. One could feel their joints pulling out as we dragged them. They were held together only by their clothing.

"I can stand rotten beefsteak, and do not mind decomposed animals, but decayed human eyes, arms, legs, and rotted human brains are too much. My insides were trying to get out through my throat, all at the same time. Burying the dead under these conditions was a difficult task. We would never risk our lives to bury them were it not for the awful smell.

"We succeeded in covering up those that were under our noses, and that without bothering to identify them. Those who helped thus bury the dead know how perfectly insincere are the various proposals that were made to bring back the dead from France. There was and is no possible way of identifying thousands of them.

"The shrapnel tore holes right through my pack. My blankets and clothing were as though a rat had gnawed a hole from one end to the other. We rifled all the packs of the dead, both of the Germans and the Americans. We had to, to live. I almost went mad before I got out of that wood."

The hunting lodge in Belleau Wood was scarred and blackened by shellfire. Wooden stubs were all that remained of the century-old woods. *Col. William Anderson USMC (Ret.)*

A Marine hunkers down in a foxhole left after the battle.
Marine Corps History Division

By dawn the situation had improved. Shearer was securely tied in on both flanks, and American artillery was active all along his front. The Germans had no intention of launching a counterattack; they were busy digging in, expecting the Americans to continue the attack. Marine patrols scoured the woods for enemy holdouts. One detail, according to Asprey, "found the hunting lodge still standing, its octagonal façade scarred by a 155mm shell, which left its entrance covered with seven dead mangled German bodies; the torso of one rested in the crotch of a nearby tree."

Shearer's men cautiously advanced to the northernmost edge of the woods without encountering any remaining enemy. The exhausted battalion commander received the welcome news and immediately sent a message to Harbord: "Woods now U.S. Marine Corps entirely.—Major Maurice Shearer."

On June 30, General Degoutte, commanding the French Sixth Army, sent the following message: "In view of the brilliant conduct of the 4th Brigade of the 2nd U.S. Division, which, in a spirited fight, took Bouresches and the important strong point of Bois de Belleau, stubbornly defended by a large enemy force, the General Commanding the Sixth Army orders that henceforth, in all official papers the Bois de Belleau shall be named, 'Bois de la Brigade des Marines.' "

General Barnett expressed his pride in the brigade's accomplishments in a congratulatory letter: "[M]y heartfelt gratitude is expressed to every officer and every man of the Fourth Brigade for the magnificent manner in which the Flag and Globe, Anchor and Eagle, have been borne against the enemy. I know what sacrifices have been made, what superhuman efforts have been put forth by every Marine, what the cost has been in death and suffering. But the high price the Marines have paid is not greater than the glory they have won."

Brigadier General S. L. A. Marshall, the great army historian, wrote, "Belleau Wood was just one of those things, like Lexington and the Alamo, an accident that changed the face of history. From the first blow both sides remained absolutely committed and the German Crown Prince, who commanded the army group, was a little foolish to let it happen that way. He was hazarding the highest possible stakes in a local dog fight and he had picked the wrong people. The Marine Brigade became, because it was unique, a little raft of sea soldiers in an ocean of the army, was without doubt the most aggressive body of die-hards on the western front."

One Marine wrote, "We engaged in the hardest kind of intensive training. . . . It was winter, the weather was cold and often stormy, but this did not make any difference. We were subject to rush calls during the night, such as forced marches to the trenches, occupations and relief, patrol work, gas and raid signals, sham raids, and other details of trench warfare. When we got through we were as hard as nails."

Belleau Wood was an awful place, more abattoir then forest preserve. It was a place of savagery and cruelty, where men killed without mercy, without compunction. It was where German machine gunners savaged the Marine Brigade—where hundreds fell to their murderous fire—while other hundreds pushed forward to close with their killers. It was the site of unequaled heroics and unspeakable horror. It pitted rifle and bayonet against automatic weapons and hand grenades—youth and inexperience against battle-hardened veteran— élan against stubborn defense. Belleau Wood became much more than a bloody battlefield for the men of the Marine Brigade; it became hallowed ground, synonymous with valor and self-sacrifice and a reference point by which to judge all other events in their lives.

Bibliography

Asprey, Robert B. *At Belleau Wood*. New York: Putnam, 1965.

Baker, Ray Stannard. *Woodrow Wilson: Life and Letters Tracing War 1915–1917*. New York: Doubleday and Company, 1937.

Berry, Henry. *Make the Kaiser Dance: Living Memories of a Forgotten War, The American Experience in World War I*. New York: Doubleday & Company, 1978.

Botting, Douglas. *The U-Boats*. Alexandria, VA: Time-Life Books, 1979.

Brannen, Carl Andrew. *Over There: A Marine in the Great War*. College Station, TX: Texas A & M University Press, 1996.

Bullard, Robert Lee. *Personalities and Reminiscences of the War*. Garden City, NJ: Doubleday, Page and Company, 1925.

Camp, Richard D. *Leatherneck Legends: Conversations with the Marine Corps' Old Breed*. St. Paul, MN: Zenith Press, 2006.

Catlin, Albertus W. *With the Help of God and a Few Marines*. New York: Doubleday, Page & Company, 1919.

Clark, George B. *Devil Dogs: Fighting Marines of World War I*. Novato, CA: Presidio Press, 1999.

Cowing, Kemper F., and Courtney R. Cooper. *Dear Folks at Home: The Glorious Story of the United States Marines in France as Told by Their Letters from the Battlefield*. New York: Houghton Mifflin Company, 1919.

Evans, Martin M. *American Voices of World War I: Primary Source Documents 1917–1920*. London: Fitzroy Publisher, 2001.

Fredericks, Pierce G. *The Great Adventure: America in the First World War*. New York: E.P. Dutton & Co., 1960.

Gibbons, Floyd. *And They Thought We Wouldn't Fight*. New York: George H. Doran Company, 1918.

Hallas, James H. *Doughboy War: The American Expeditionary Force in World War I*. Boulder, CO: Lynne Rienner, 2000.

Hamilton, Craig and Louise Corbin (ed.). *Echoes from Over There: By the Men of the Army and Marine Corps Who Fought in France*. New York: The Soldiers Publishing Company, 1919.

Harbord, Maj. Gen. James G. *Leaves from a War Diary*. New York: Dodd, Mead & Company, 1926.

Harries, Meirion and Susie. *The Last Days of Innocence: America at War, 1917–1918*. New York: Random House, 1997.

Heinl, Robert Debs, Jr. *Soldiers of the Sea: The U.S. Marine Corps, 1775–1962*. Annapolis: United States Naval Institute, 1962.

Hemrick, Levi E. *Once a Marine*. New York: Carlton Press, Inc., 1968.

Heyman, Neil M. *Daily Life During World War I*. Westport, CT: Greenwood Press, 2002.

Jackson, Warren R. *His Time in Hell: A Texas Marine in France*. Novato, CA: Presidio Press, 2001.

Lewis, Charles L. *Famous American Marines*. Boston, MA: L. C. Page & Company, 1950.

Mackin, Elton E. *Suddenly We Didn't Want to Die: Memoirs of a World War I Marine*. Novato, CA: Presidio Press, 1993.

Marshall, S. L. A. *World War I*. New York: American Heritage Press, 1964.

McClellan, Maj. Edwin N. "The Fourth Brigade of Marines in the Training Areas and the Operations in the Verdun Sector," *Marine Corps Gazette*, March 1920.

———. "Operations of the Fourth Brigade of Marines in the Aisne Defensive," *Marine Corps Gazette*, March 1920

———. "Capture of Hill 142, Battle of Belleau Wood, and Capture of Bouresches," *Marine Corps Gazette*, September 1920.

———. "The Battle of Belleau Wood," *Marine Corps Gazette*, December 1920.

———. "A Brief History of the Fourth Brigade of Marines," *Marine Corps Gazette*, December 1919.

Morgan, Daniel E. *When the World Went Mad: A Thrilling Story of the Late War, Told in the Language of the Trenches*. Pike, NH: The Brass Hat, 1993.

Roosevelt, Theodore. *Rank and File: True Stories of the Great War*. New York: Charles Scribner's Sons, 1928.

Stallings, Laurence. *The Doughboys; The Story of the AEF, 1917–1918*. New York: Harper & Row, 1963.

Thomason, Capt. John W. *Fix Bayonets!* New York: Charles Scribner's Sons, 1925.

Toland, John. *No Man's Land 1918: The Last Year of the Great War*. New York: Doubleday & Company, Inc. 1980.

Turner, Martha Anne. *The World of Colonel John W. Thomason USMC*. Austin, TX: Eakin Press, 1984.

Vorst, B. Van. *France Our Ally: A Brief Account of France, Its People, and Their Pride in the War, with Special Information for American Soldiers*. New York: Association Press, 1918.

Archival Sources

Located at Quantico, Virginia, the Marine Corps University archives, which are maintained by the Alfred M. Gray Marine Corps Research Center, provide a rich source of material for researchers of Marine Corps history including nearly four thousand collections of papers donated by active duty and former officers and enlisted men, documenting every conflict involving Marines. Of particular importance to this book were the oral histories that have been conducted by the Marine Corps History Division over the years.

Blake, Maj. Gen. Robert. Marine Corps Historical Division, Oral History Interview, 1973.

Bleasdale, Brig. Gen. Victor F. Marine Corps Historical Division, Oral History Interview, 1984.

Cates, Gen. Clifton B. Marine Corps Historical Division, Oral History Interview, 1973.

———. Personal Observations of the Taking of Bouresches.

Erskine, Gen. Graves B. Marine Corps Historical Division, Oral History Interview, 1975.

Gaspar, Lt. Col. Walter S. Marine Corps Historical Division, Oral History Interview, 1976.

Krulewitch, Maj. Gen. Melvin L. Marine Corps Historical Division, Oral History Interview, 1974.

Noble, Gen. Alfred H. Marine Corps Historical Division, Oral History Interview, 1973.

Paradis, Gunnery Sgt. Don V. Marine Corps Historical Division, Oral History Interview, 1973.

Thomas, Gen. Gerald C. Marine Corps Historical Division, Oral History Interview, 1973.

Worton, Maj. Gen. William A. Marine Corps Historical Division, Oral History Interview, 1973.

Personal Interviews

Lemuel C. Shepherd
Edward A. Craig
Robert A. Benedict

Unpublished Manuscript

Second Division Northwest of Chateau Thierry: 1 June–10 July, 1918.

Military Publications

United States Army in the World War 1917–1919: Military Operations of the American Expeditionary Forces. Historical Division, Department of the Army, Wash: GPO 1948.

The Medical Department of the United States Navy with the Army and Marine Corps in World War I. Department of the Navy, Wash: GPO 1948.

Illustrations

Tomlinson, Everett T. *Sergeant Ted Cole, United States Marines.* New York: Houghton Mifflin Company, 1919.

Index

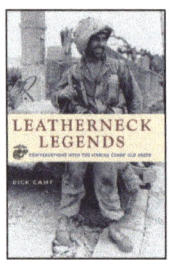

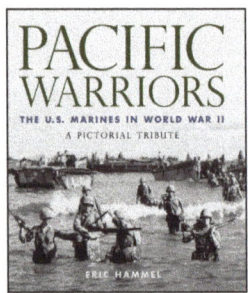
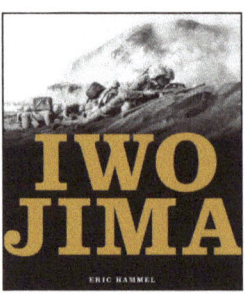

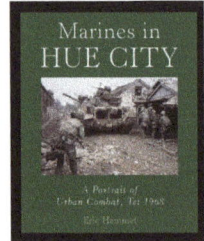
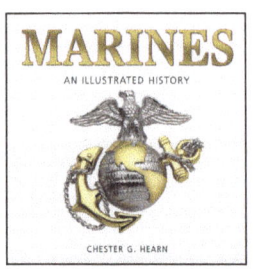
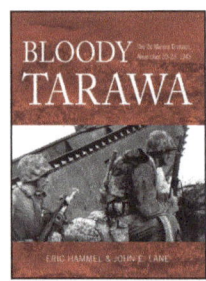

CPSIA information can be obtained
at www.ICGtesting.com
Printed in the USA
LVHW072007021222
734471LV00009B/257

9 780760 331897